ST PET

MARC BENNETTS

EYEWITNESS TRAVEL

Left **Russian ballet** Right **The Hermitage**

LONDON, NEW YORK,
MELBOURNE, MUNICH AND DELHI
www.dk.com

Design, Editorial and Picture Research,
by Quadrum Solutions, Krishnamai,
33B, Sir Pochkanwala Road, Worli,
Mumbai, India

Reproduced by Colourscan, Singapore
Printed and bound in China by Leo
Paper Products Ltd

First published in Great Britain in 2008
by Dorling Kindersley Limited
80 Strand, London WC2R 0RL
A Penguin Company

**Copyright 2008 © Dorling
Kindersley Limited, London**

A CIP catalogue record is available from
the British Library.

ISBN 978 1 4053 2941 5

Within each Top 10 list in this book, no
hierarchy of quality or popularity is
implied. All 10 are, in the editor's
opinion, of roughly equal merit.

Contents

St Petersburg's Top 10

The information in this DK Eyewitness Top 10 Travel Guide is checked regularly.
Every effort has been made to ensure that this book is as up-to-date as possible at the time of
going to press. Some details, however, such as telephone numbers, opening hours, prices,
gallery hanging arrangements and travel information are liable to change. The publishers
cannot accept responsibility for any consequences arising from the use of this book, nor for
any material on third party websites, and cannot guarantee that any website address in this
book will be a suitable source of travel information. We value the views and suggestions of
our readers very highly. Please write to: Publisher, DK Eyewitness Travel Guides,
Dorling Kindersley, 80 Strand, London, Great Britain WC2R 0RL.

Left *Matryoshka* dolls Centre **Statue of Pushkin** Right **Cruiser** *Aurora*

Contents

Left **Catherine Palace, Tsarkoe Selo** Right **The interiors of the Alexandriinskiy Theatre**

Key to abbreviations
Adm *admission charge*

ST PETERSBURG'S TOP 10

ST PETERSBURG'S TOP 10

TOP 10 St Petersburg's Highlights

From the pre-revolutionary grandeur of the Hermitage and the Mariinskiy Theatre to the ubiquitous reminders of the country's Soviet period, St Petersburg is a city where eras, and architectural styles, collide. Blessed with some of the world's most magnificent skylines, the city has been the inspiration for many of Russia's greatest writers, from Gogol to Dostoevsky. Known throughout the country as "The Venice of the North", Russia's second city is a place of wonder and enigma, of "White Nights" and long, freezing winters.

1 Nevskiy Prospekt

The cultural heart of the city, this area is home to many of the top sights, including the Cathedral of Our Lady of Kazan *(see pp8–9)*.

2 Hermitage

This opulent former residence of the tsars contains one of the world's largest art collections, boasting masterpieces by Leonardo da Vinci and Michelangelo *(see pp10–13)*.

3 Church on Spilled Blood

The twisted, colourful domes of this church make it one of the city's most famous landmarks *(see pp14–15)*.

4 Mariinskiy Theatre

Russia is famed for its ballet and opera, and the lavish auditorium of this theatre is the perfect place to witness a performance *(see pp16–17)*.

5 Russian Museum

This museum features a wide range of Russian art, including the works of Bryullov and Repin *(see pp18–19)*.

Previous pages **Church on Spilled Blood**

Peter and Paul Fortress

6 The history of the city dates from the founding of the fortress in 1703. It was originally intended to defend the city against Swedish invaders *(see pp20–21).*

St Isaac's Cathedral

7 The largest church in Russia, the construction of the cathedral took 40 years to complete. Its interiors, such as the detailed ceiling paintings, survived shelling during World War II *(see pp22–3).*

Peterhof

8 With its Great Palace and magnificent landscaped gardens, Peterhof perfectly encapsulates the extravagance of tsarist Russia. Located 30 km (19 miles) west of St Petersburg, it is the ideal destination for an excursion *(see pp24–5).*

Tsarskoe Selo

9 A fine example of tsarist architectural grandeur, Tsarskoe Selo, with its lavish imperial palace and beautiful parks, is the perfect place to spend a relaxing day *(see pp26–7).*

Pavlovsk

10 In 1777, Catherine the Great presented Pavlovsk to her son, the future tsar Paul 1. Today it is a romantic cluster of ruins dotted around a charming palace *(see pp28–9).*

🔟 Nevskiy Prospekt

A stroll along Nevskiy prospekt is a journey through time, from tsarist-era splendours to the cafés and chic boutiques of modern-day St Petersburg. Immortalised in Russian literature, this 4.5-km (3-mile) stretch has been the hub of the city's social life since the 18th century. If, in Europe, all roads lead to Rome, then in St Petersburg they converge on Nevskiy. Home to numerous fine churches and monuments, this is an ideal starting point for an exploration of the city. Many of St Petersburg's most famous sights, such as the unforgettable Cathedral of Our Lady of Kazan, are just a short walk away

Siege Plaque

🚶 Nevskiy prospekt is a very busy street, so make sure to use the frequent *perekhodi* (underpasses), indicated by signs showing a flight of steps.

🍽 There are dozens of cafés along Nevskiy prospekt, as well as countless ice-cream vendors. Try the city's famous ice cream – Dasha and Mitya.

• Map L3–P4 • www.nevsky-prospekt.com
• Cathedral of Our Lady Of Kazan: 317 5856; open 9am–7:30pm
• Armenian Church: 318 4108; open 9am–9pm
• Gostinyy Dvor: 710 5408; open 10am–10pm
• Waxworks, Beloselskiy-Belozerskiy Palace: 312 3644; open noon–6pm
• Church of St Catherine: open 9am–9pm
• Stroganov Palace: 312 9054; open 10am–6pm Wed–Mon; Adm: adults 300 roubles; children 150 roubles • Russian National Library: 310 7137; 9am–9pm Mon–Fri, 11am–7pm Sat & Sun

Top 10 Features

1 Cathedral of Our Lady of Kazan
2 Siege Plaque
3 Armenian Church
4 Gostinyy Dvor
5 Beloselskiy-Belozerskiy Palace
6 Catherine the Great's Statue
7 Church of St Catherine
8 Stroganov Palace
9 Gogol Statue
🔟 Russian National Library

Cathedral of Our Lady of Kazan

This cathedral (1811) *(see p59)* was inspired by St Peter's Basilica in Rome. It was used as a museum of atheism during the Soviet period – religious services made a return only in 1992.

Siege Plaque

Dating from the years of the WWII siege of the city *(see p32)*, the plaque reads, "Citizens! This side of the street is more dangerous during an artillery bombardment!"

Armenian Church

This pretty blue and white church (1780) *(left)* was designed by Catherine the Great's court architect, Yuriy Velten. A crumbling, forgotten ruin during the Soviet period, the "Blue Pearl of Nevskiy prospekt" has recently been returned to St Petersburg's Armenian community.

4 Gostinyy Dvor

This striking arcade *(left)* has been the focal point of the city's shopping since the mid-18th century. It houses a vast array of shops as well as a number of cafés.

5 Beloselskiy-Belozerskiy Palace

This palace (1847–8) *(below)*, now a waxworks museum, was once home to one of Rasputin's murderers *(see p74)*. It later served as the Soviet-era head-quarters of the Communist Party.

6 Catherine the Great's Statue

Catherine the Great *(see p13)* was a German princess who came to power in Russia after an imperial coup in 1762, during which her husband, Peter III was murdered. This is the only statue of her in the city *(right)*.

7 Church of St Catherine

This is the oldest Roman Catholic church in Russia. An 18th-century mixture of Baroque and Neo-Classical styles, it can hold up to 2,500 people.

8 Stroganov Palace

This Baroque-style palace once had an exhibition devoted to the evils of the aristo-cracy. The building now belongs to the Russian Museum *(see pp18–19)*.

9 Gogol Statue

Many of Nikolai Gogol's stories are set among the city's streets *(see p34)*. This statue (1997), created by Mikhail Belov, is a fitting tribute to his troubled genius.

10 Russian National Library

This is Russia's oldest state library *(left)*. Hous-ing around 33 million items, it also boasts the oldest handwritten book in the Russian language, dating from 1057.

Origins

Originally known as the "Great Prospective Road," Nevskiy prospekt was cut through thick forest in 1718. Prone to flooding, the stretch lay unused and was home to packs of wolves for many years. The area takes its current name from Alexander Nevskiy, a 13th-century national hero who defeated invading Swedish and Danish armies.

🔟 The Hermitage

This grand ensemble of buildings, located on the bank of the Neva river, houses one of the world's greatest art collections. Built up by successive tsars, the museum boasts priceless masterpieces by Picasso and Rembrandt, as well as exhibits devoted to prehistoric, Classical and Oriental art. The Hermitage also contains the Winter Palace, the pre-revolutionary residence of the tsars, and the headquarters for the Provisional Government after the initial 1917 Revolution (see p32). It has been said that it would take a visitor 11 years to examine every one of the Hermitage's exhibits.

The granite Atlantes

🗝 For a breathtaking and original view of the Hermitage, step off Nevskiy prospekt and, sticking to the left-hand side, follow Bolshaya Morskaya ulitsa to its very end – as the street bends round to the arch of the General Staff Building, the Hermitage is revealed in all its glory.

🍴 As a visit to the Hermitage can easily take up an entire day, it is a good idea to have lunch on the premises, making use of the café on the ground floor.

• Map L2
• Dvortsovaya nab. 30–8
• 710 9079
• Open 10:30am–6pm Tue–Sat, 10:30am–5pm Sun
• Adm: 350 roubles; free on first Thu of every month
• www.hermitage museum.org

Top 10 Features
1. Palace Square
2. Winter Palace
3. The Old Hermitage
4. The New Hermitage
5. General Staff Building
6. Alexander Column
7. Pavilion Hall
8. Winter Palace State Rooms
9. Raphael Loggias
10. Atlantes

Palace Square
This imposing square, designed by Carlo Rossi, overlooks the Hermitage's main entrance *(right)*. The setting for the Bloody Sunday massacre of 1905, *(see p32)*, the square today often hosts concerts and demonstrations.

Winter Palace
The opulent Winter Palace *(below)* was built for Tsarina Elizabeth between 1754–62. It contains the Malachite Room, decorated with over two tonnes of ornamental stone, and architect Rastrelli's masterpiece, the Main Staircase.

The Old Hermitage
Designed by Yuriy Velten, the impressive Old Hermitage was constructed between 1771–87 to house Catherine the Great's growing collection of paintings. It was opened as a public museum by Nicholas I in 1852.

It is a good idea to book your tickets on the Hermitage website – this will save you having to queue on the day.

The New Hermitage

4 This building *(above)* was specifically designed as a museum because of Nicholas I's desire to make the exhibits more accessible to the public.

General Staff Building

5 This landmark building's two wings are connected by a magnificent double arch topped by Victory in her chariot (1892).

Alexander Column

6 This column is the world's largest freestanding monument. Dedicated to Alexander I, it was erected in 1834.

Pavilion Hall

7 This gold and white hall *(above)* has striking marble columns and crystal chandeliers. It houses James Cox's Peacock Clock, which was once owned by Prince Grigory Potemkin, Catherine's secret husband.

Winter Palace State Rooms

8 These rooms *(right)* were designed for state ceremonies. The St George Hall is used for state meetings even today.

Raphael Loggias

9 This corridor *(left)* is a copy of the Vatican's famous 16th-century gallery. It depicts 52 chronologically arranged biblical scenes.

Atlantes

10 Ten 5-m (16-ft) tall granite Atlantes prop up the former public entrance to the Hermitage. It is a tradition to rub the toe of one of them and make a wish.

The Hermitage Under Siege

The Hermitage came under frequent attack during the WWII siege *(see p32)*. The Nazis had pledged to "completely destroy Leningrad" (as St Petersburg was then known), and the Hermitage soon became a symbol of the city's resistance. Although many museum workers died of starvation, and snow piled up inside its lavish halls, the Hermitage continued to support the city's cultural life.

Ninety-nine per cent of the Hermitage is dedicated to foreign art. Major works of Russian art are in the Russian Museum (see pp18–19).

11

Left **Rubens'** *Bacchus* Centre **Gauguin's** *Woman with Fruit* Right **Rembrandt's** *Abraham's Sacrifice*

Hermitage Works of Art

1 Madonna Litta
Leonardo da Vinci's *Madonna Litta* (c.1491) is a powerful work that was often copied by his contemporaries. It is one of two paintings by the artist in this museum, the other being *Benois Madonna*.

2 Abraham's Sacrifice
This 17th-century masterpiece by Rembrandt depicts the dramatic moment in the Old Testament when an angel prevents Abraham from sacrificing his son to God.

3 Bacchus
Bacchus (1638–40), by Peter Paul Rubens, depicts the Roman god of wine and intoxication as a bloated, obese man, wholly abandoned to his own pleasure. The painting was part of a private collection acquired by the Hermitage in 1772.

Leonardo da Vinci's *Madonna Litta*

4 Music
Music was created by Henri Matisse in 1910 for Sergey Shchukin's Moscow mansion. The painting, which depicts bright red figures lost in their own world, was denounced as barbaric at the time due to its evocative rendering of abandonment and spontaneity.

5 Three Women
Picasso's *Three Women* (1908) is a precursor to the Cubist style that developed in France between 1908 and 1914. There is a distinct African influence in the bold use of colour and the faces of the women, which are inspired by tribal masks.

6 St John the Divine in Silence
A rare example of Russian art in the Hermitage, this icon (1679) was created by a painter from the Kirillo-Byelozyorsk monastery in Arkhangelsk. It depicts St John in deep contemplation of the bible with his hand touching his lips – a sign that he is keeping silence in accordance with his holy vow. The icon's date and place of creation is recorded on its reverse.

Catherine the Great

Catherine the Great (left), a self-confessed "glutton for art", came to power in Russia in 1762. In 1764, she made the first significant purchases for the Hermitage. This initial batch of paintings – 225 works of European art bought from a German merchant – is generally regarded as the birth of the Hermitage as an art gallery. From this point on, large-scale purchases of art became the norm, as Russian ambassadors and envoys were ordered to build up the collection, buying in bulk from impoverished English, Italian and Dutch aristocratic families. The tsarina's personal favourites were works by Rubens and Leonardo.

Whatever its meaning, there is no denying the energy contained in the figure's pose.

St Sebastian
St Sebastian was created by Titian in 1576, towards the end of his life, when he painted what are widely considered to be his most moving works. He applied the paint with his fingers or a palette knife and this, coupled with the deep colours employed, produces a dramatic effect.

Statue of Voltaire
The statue of Voltaire dates from 1781, and is Jean-Antoine Houdon's most famous work. The lifelike face of the philosopher shows a remarkable depth of characterization. The sculpture was prepared from life studies that took place when Voltaire visited Paris in 1778.

Woman with Fruit
This painting is representative of Gauguin's work during his stay in the French Polynesian Islands in the 1890s. The bright colours and flowing lines evoke a tropical paradise – some say the woman carrying fruit symbolizes Eve in the Garden of Eden.

Key
Ground Floor
First Floor
Second Floor

Crouching Boy
The meaning of Michelangelo's marble sculpture has been a source of contention among scholars over the years. Some believe the figure is a grieving man or a conquered soldier, others say that it represents a soul yet to be born.

By the time of her death, Catherine the Great's art collection was far larger than anything owned by any other European monarch.

🔟 Church on Spilled Blood

The Church on Spilled Blood, a cacophony of colour just off Nevskiy prospekt, stands out in St Petersburg by nature of its Russian Revival style, something that is extremely rare in this city of Baroque and Neo-Classical architecture. Designed by Alfred Parland and Ignatiy Malyshev, the church, which is sometimes referred to as "Saviour on Blood", was built as a memorial to Alexander II in 1881 on the site of his assassination. The interior opened to the public in 1997, after over 20 years of restoration.

Mosaic wall detail

Marble window frames

⭐ Lovers of Soviet memorabilia *(see p46)* should pay a visit to the Souvenir Market located opposite the church.

🍴 After visiting the church, if the weather is good, head off to the Mikhaylovskiy Garden nearby for a picnic lunch.

• Map N2
• Konyushennya ploshchad
• 315 1636
• Open May–Sep: 10am–7pm, Oct–Apr: 11am–6pm; closed Wed
• Adm: 300 roubles (for non-Russians)
• http://eng.cathedral.ru/saviour

Top 10 Features

1. Mosaic Walls
2. Mosaic Portraits of Saints
3. Window Frames
4. Plaques commemorating Alexander II's reign
5. Mosaic Tympanum
6. Steeple
7. Bell Tower Coat of Arms
8. Icons
9. Shrine marking the exact spot where Alexander II was slain
10. Exhibition on the restoration of the church

Mosaic Walls
The church has over 7,000 sq m (75,300 sq ft) of mosaics covering its interior and exterior. A wide range of materials, including jasper, porphyry and Italian marble, have been used to create these lavish artworks.

Mosaic Portraits of Saints
Colourful mosaic portraits *(left)* of biblical saints, laid out in rows of *kokoshniki* gables (tiered decorative arches), adorn the exterior of the church.

Window Frames
The window frames are carved out of marble transported from Estonia and cast in the form of traditional decorative patterns.

During the Siege (see p32), the church was used to store potatoes, which gave rise to its nickname, "Saviour on Potatoes"

4 Plaques commemorating Alexander II's reign

The perimeter of the lower wall has 20 dark-red plaques made of Norwegian granite, which illustrate key events of the 25-year reign of Alexander II (1855–81), including the emancipation of the serfs in 1861.

5 Mosaic Tympanum

The exterior of the church is made up of panels depicting scenes from the New Testament. During the Siege (see p32), starving citizens gathered to pray under the Tympanum (above), finding solace in its depiction of Christ on His throne.

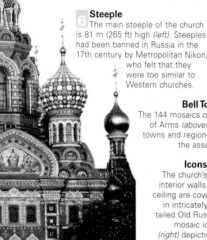

6 Steeple

The main steeple of the church is 81 m (265 ft) high (left). Steeples had been banned in Russia in the 17th century by Metropolitan Nikon, who felt that they were too similar to Western churches.

7 Bell Tower Coat of Arms

The 144 mosaics on the Bell Tower Coat of Arms (above) represent the provinces, towns and regions of Russia at the time of the assassination of Alexander II.

8 Icons

The church's interior walls and ceiling are covered in intricately detailed Old Russian mosaic icons (right) depicting a vast array of biblical figures and scenes.

9 Shrine marking the exact spot where Alexander II was slain

Decorated with images of the tsar's patron saint, the shrine was designed by Alfred Parland and completed in 1907. It was restored in the mid-1990s.

10 Exhibition on the restoration of the church

This is a fascinating exhibition depicting the state of the church prior to its restoration in the 1990s. Look out for the section of Alexander II's shrine that has been left in its previous condition to demonstrate the scale of the restorative work carried out on the detailed mosaics (right).

A Church in Honour of the Tsar

The Church on Spilled Blood has never been used for weddings, funerals or any other church services. It was intended to be entirely dedicated to the memory of Alexander II, although some sermon readings did take place before the revolution.

⑩ Mariinskiy Theatre

The Mariinskiy Theatre has long been one of the world's most respected venues for opera and ballet. It has seen premieres by such greats as Tchaikovsky and Prokofiev, while the dance school attached to it produced Nureyev and Nijinsky. When it was first opened to the public in 1860, the Mariinskiy boasted the largest stage in the world. Known as the Kirov Theatre of Opera and Ballet throughout much of the Soviet era, the Mariinskiy reverted to its original name in 1992. The theatre is a St Petersburg institution, and a visit here is a highlight of any trip to the city.

Ticket for a show

🌀 Russians tend to dress up when attending the ballet or the opera. While a suit and tie or ballroom dress are not strictly necessary, guests should make an effort to fit in.

💬 After the show, Za Tsenoi, or the Irish bar Shamrock *(see p78)*, are good places to discuss the performance over dinner.

• Map B5
• Teatralnaya ploschad 1
• 326 4141
• Performances usually begin at 11:30am (matinee) or 7pm.
• Tickets are more expensive for tourists than Russians and can cost anything from 500 roubles to 3,500.
• www.mariinsky.ru

Performances

1 A performance here *(right)* is one that will stay with you for a long time. Not to be missed are Tchaikovsky's *Eugene Onegin* and Mussorgsky's *Boris Godunov*. Also look out for opera stars Anna Netrebko, Olga Borodina and Vladimir Galuzin.

Stage

2 Designed in 1914 by Aleksandr Golovin during Russian Ballet's golden age, this luxuriant stage curtain *(above)* has revealed, and then concealed, countless world-famous ballet dancers.

Façade

3 The Neo-Renaissance façade *(below)* was remodelled in 1883–6 by Viktor Schröter, who added most of the ornamental detail.

Za Tsenoi

4 "Za Tsenoi" means "backstage" and this restaurant *(see p76)*, located a few steps away from the venue, aims to recreate the atmosphere of the theatre. Serving a mixed European and Russian menu, this is the perfect place both to savour fine food and recall the show.

Tickets for top performances, such as Swan Lake, can sell out very quickly.

5 Royal Box
The Royal Box, with its imperial eagles *(above)*, lustrous curtains and sparkling chandeliers, offers a vivid reminder of Imperial Russia. The tsars regularly watched performances from here.

6 New Mariinskiy Stage
The Mariinskiy II, designed by Dominique Perrault, will be located directly behind the current theatre and will seat 2,000. Due to open in 2009, the new stage will be linked to the original Mariinskiy by a bridge over the Kryukov Canal.

7 Ceiling
Don't forget to take a look at the Mariinskiy's intricate ceiling *(above)*. Dating from 1856 and designed by the Italian artist Enrico Franchioli, it depicts dancing girls and cupids.

8 Programme
A programme of the event *(above)* will make for a beautiful souvenir. Available in English and Russian, the programmes are sold in the foyer and at the ticket desk.

Nureyev's Defection
After the 1917 Revolution, many of the Mariinskiy's ballet dancers defected to other countries. Rudolf Nureyev left in 1961. Having broken the rules about mingling with foreigners and under pressure from the KGB for his open homosexuality, he finally defected while on tour in France in 1961, becoming an immediate success in the West.

9 Audiences
The theatre is a fine place for people-spotting. Those with an interest in the Russian government and showbiz may be lucky enough to spot celebrities from the worlds of politics and entertainment.

10 Theatre Square
Once known as Carousel Square, Theatre Square *(above)* and the surrounding canal-lined streets have long been the home of the city's artistic community.

Tickets are usually always available from touts on the day of the show, albeit for vastly inflated prices.

🔟 Russian Museum

While the Hermitage is home to art collected from all over the world, the Russian Museum is an exclusively Russian affair, its exhibits ranging from priceless 12th-century icons to the avant-garde paintings of Kandinsky and Malevich. Opened to the public for the first time in 1898, the museum was nationalised after the 1917 Revolution and its collection swelled by works confiscated from palaces and churches. From the 1930s until Gorbachev's restructuring (see p32), however, it exhibited mainly Socialist Realism art. The museum is housed in the 19th-century Mikhaylovskiy Palace, one of the finest Neo-Classical creations of Carlo Rossi, the Italian architect also responsible for Palace Square (see p10).

Russian Museum's façade

⊙ It is worth buying an audio guide to accompany you on your visit to the museum. These are available in English and can be hired at the ticket office.

⊖ After visiting the museum, try some real Russian pancakes *(blinis)* in the restaurant/café on the ground floor.

- Map N3
- Inzhenernaya ulitsa 4
- 595 4248
- Open 10am–5pm Mon, 10am–4pm Wed–Sun; closed Tue
- Adm: adults 300 roubles; children 150 roubles
- Disabled visitors call 314 6424
- www.rusmuseum.ru

Top 10 Features

1. The Last Day of Pompeii
2. The Zaporozhye Cossacks Writing a Mocking Letter to the Turkish Sultan
3. Perfected Portrait of Ivan Kliun
4. Knight at the Crossroads
5. Descent into Hell Icon
6. Pine Grove
7. Living Head
8. Wrestlers
9. Portrait of the Poetess Anna Akhmatova
10. Old Russian Decorative and Applied Art

1 The Last Day of Pompeii
One of the first Russian paintings to attract attention abroad, Karl Bryullov's (1799–1852) magnificent creation *(above)* was the result of his visit to Pompeii immediately after an eruption of Mount Vesuvius in 1828.

Key
First floor
Ground floor

2 The Zaporozhye Cossacks Writing a Mocking Letter to the Turkish Sultan
Ilya Repin's colossal piece is based on the Ukrainian Cossacks' fight with Turkey in the 17th century.

3 Perfected Portrait of Ivan Kliun
This distorted portrait, by leading avant-garde painter, Kazmir Malevich (1878–1935), is a typical example of his obsession with simple geometric shapes.

Knight at the Crossroads

A symbol of Russia's uncertain future at the fin-de-siècle, Viktor Vasnetsov's (1848–1926) brooding and mournful knight *(right)* deserves to be seen as more than mere allegory. The hyper-realistic painting is remarkable for its imaginative use of colour.

Descent into Hell Icon

Created sometime in the 15th century, this icon, which survived the anti-religion purges after the 1917 Revolution, has been attributed to the Pskov school of icon painters.

Pine Grove

Ivan Shishkin (1832–98), a contemporary of the Wanderers *(see p84)*, was renowned for his soothing forest landscapes. The serene *Pine Grove* is a classic example of his desire to depict nature in its pure, unadorned beauty.

Living Head

Despite having his work suppressed by the Soviets, Pavel Filonov (1883–1941) refused to sell any of his heavily detailed paintings, such as *Living Head*, to foreign collectors. A contemporary and close acquaintance of the writer Daniil Kharms *(see p34)*, Filonov perished during the siege of the city *(see p32)*.

Wrestlers

Natalia Goncharova (1881–1962), who had links to the Pushkin family *(see p34)*, was deeply inspired by the primitivism of Russian folk art. She was also an accomplished costume designer. *Wrestlers* (1908–09) is an example of her welding of cubism and pre-revolutionary Russian avant-garde.

Museum Guide

The museum's exhibits are arranged chronologically, starting with the icons on the first floor. The exhibition then descends to the ground floor of the main building and Rossi Wing, and then back up to the first floor of the Benois Wing. Exhibitions are changed regularly.

Old Russian Decorative and Applied Art

This section of the museum has a collection of porcelain, furniture, glass and fascinating artifacts *(above)* that has been built up since 1895.

Portrait of the Poetess Anna Akhmatova

Anna Akhmatova's *(see p34)* portrait, by Russian Cubist painter Nathan Altman (1889–1970), was completed in 1914, when Akhmatova was 25.

Peter and Paul Fortress

First built in wood, and later reconstructed block by block in stone, the Peter and Paul Fortress dates from the founding of St Petersburg in 1703. During its construction, hundreds of serfs and Swedish prisoners of war perished in the murderous swamps that surrounded it. Containing a magnificent cathedral, dark, damp cells, a popular beach and fine examples of Baroque architecture, the fortress, like the city itself, is a contradictory wonder that at times exhilarates and, at times, chills the bones.

The Mint's façade

It is worth setting aside an entire morning or afternoon for a visit to the fortress, and longer if you want to sunbathe on the riverside beach.

There are many cafés on the territory of the fortress. However, during summer, it is ideal to take a picnic and relax on the beach.

- Map C2
- Petropavlovskaya krepost
- 232 9454
- Open summer: 10am–6pm Thu–Mon, 10am–5pm Tue; winter: 11am–6pm Thu–Mon, 11am–5pm Tue
- Adm: adults 170 roubles; children 80 roubles
- www.spbmuseum.ru

Top 10 Features

1. St Peter's Gate
2. Cathedral of SS Peter and Paul
3. Neva Gate
4. Trubetskoy Bastion
5. Statue of Peter the Great
6. Commandant's House
7. The Mint
8. The Grand Ducal Burial Vault
9. Engineer's House
10. The Beach

St Peter's Gate
The gate (1718) depicts St Peter's banishment of the winged mystic, Simon Magus. This Baroque construction with scrolled wings allegorizes Peter the Great's victory at the Battle of Poltava in 1709.

Cathedral of SS Peter and Paul
The stylish Baroque cathedral *(right)* was a deliberate attempt by Peter the Great to commission buildings based on designs that rejected traditional Russian church architecture.

Neva Gate
Built in 1784–7, the Neva Gate *(left)* was referred to as "Death Gate" during the years it was used to transport prisoners to execution in the neighbouring Schlusselburg Fortress. The archway contains plaques that commemorate record flood levels.

High-profile prisoners who served time in the fortress include Dostoevsky, Peter the Great's son Aleksey and Lenin's brother.

Trubetskoy Bastion

The bastion's dark cells *(above)* served as a prison. The first prisoner here was Aleksey, who was accused of treason by his father, Peter the Great, and executed in 1718.

Statue of Peter the Great

Mikhail Chemiakin's statue *(right)* caused great controversy upon its unveiling in 1991. Intended to depict Peter the Great's "alter-ego", the statue portrays the founder of St Petersburg with a very tiny head and spindly fingers.

Commandant's House

A reminder of some of unpleasant aspects of the fortress's history, this early 18th-century structure *(left)* is where political prisoners were brought for interrogation during the years of tsarist rule.

The Mint

Established in the early 18th century by Peter the Great, the mint is still in use today. It is one of only two places in Russia, the other being Moscow, where coins, along with medals and badges, are minted.

The Grand Ducal Burial Vault

The vault (1908) was constructed to replace the already overflowing cathedral as the final resting place of the tsars.

Engineer's House

This building (1749), used as living quarters for engineers of the city's garrison, now houses exhibitions *(above)* dedicated to St Petersburg's pre-revolutionary days.

A Fortress Against the Swedes

The Peter and Paul Fortress was originally intended to provide protection for the new city against possible incursions and attacks by the Swedish navy. However, the Swedes were defeated even before the finishing touches had been put to the fortress. Stripped of its intended function, it was turned over to the local garrison. It also served as a prison for political dissenters.

The Beach

During summer, the beach *(right)* is full of sunbathers. In winter, it becomes the exclusive haunt of "The Walruses", a group of St Petersburg citizens who break through the thick ice to dip into the freezing waters beneath.

TOP 10 St Isaac's Cathedral

Peter the Great had originally commissioned a smaller church of the same name, much closer to the river, but this was destroyed in floods soon after its construction in 1710. The larger, present-day St Isaac's was opened in 1858, and was designed by French architect Auguste de Montferrand. The cathedral weighs 300,000 tonnes, and the engineering operation needed to erect it was, at the time, of an almost unprecedented scale. Used as a museum of atheism during the Soviet years, the cathedral, the largest in Russia, is still officially a museum, with a collection of 19th-century art.

Angels with Torch

⊘ St Isaac's is most impressive around dusk during the winter, when it dominates the snowy skyline like some giant sentinel standing guard in the vastness of St Isaac's Square.

◑ The popular café, Idiot *(see p70),* is close by and does great business lunches.

- Map K4
- Isaakievskaya ploshchad
- 315 9732
- Open May–Sep: 10am–8pm Thu–Tue; Oct–Apr: 11am–7pm Thu–Tue
- Adm: adults 300 roubles; children 170 roubles
- http://eng.cathedral.ru/isaac

Top 10 Features

1. Ceiling Painting
2. The Dome
3. St Catherine's Chapel
4. Red Granite Columns
5. Angels with Torch
6. Iconostasis
7. Statues of the Apostles
8. South Doors
9. Internal Walls
10. Traces of Nazi Bombardment

1 Ceiling Painting
"The Virgin in Majesty" (1847), the fresco that adorns the inside of the cathedral's cupola *(above),* was created by Karl Bryullov and covers an area of 816 sq m (8,780 sq ft).

2 The Dome
St Isaac's gilded viewing dome is decorated with angels created by sculptor Josef Hermann. The dome also offers breathtaking views across the city – you can see the Hermitage *(see pp10–13)* from here.

3 St Catherine's Chapel
This chapel *(left)* is remarkable for its "Resurrection" (1850–54) – a stunning hybrid of Baroque and Classical styles. Sculpted by the artist Nikolay Pimenov, it is the crowning point of the exquisite white marble iconostasis.

Peter the Great's birthday fell on 30 May, which was also St Isaac's birthday, thus making St Isaac Peter's patron saint.

4 Red Granite Columns

The 48 columns *(above)* in the cathedral were specially imported from Finland at tremendous cost and effort.

5 Angels with Torch

The reverent angels holding up the gas torches that crown the four corners of the cathedral were created by Ivan Vitali, who was also responsible for many of the other figures that adorn the cathedral.

6 Iconostasis

Three rows of icons surround the royal doors, above which is Pyotr Klodt's gilded "Christ in Majesty" *(above)*.

7 Statues of the Apostles

Statues of apostles *(below)* stand guard at the top of the cathedral. St Mark with a lion, St Matthew with an angel, St John with an eagle and St Luke with a calf are at the four points of the compass.

8 South Doors

The south portico has three great double-shuttered doors *(left)* made of cast bronze over oak and decorated with biblical scenes.

9 Internal Walls

The interiors of the cathedral are adorned with 14 different types of coloured marble and over 40 types of semi-precious stones.

10 Traces of Nazi Bombardment

St Isaac's was hit by artillery bombardment during the Siege of Leningrad *(see p32)*. Traces of this have been left on the left-hand side of the cathedral's steps as a reminder of the war years.

Human Suffering

The construction of St Isaac's Cathedral was accompanied by much suffering and sacrifice of human life. Hundreds of serfs lost their lives, crushed to death by falling chunks of marble. At least 60 people were killed by inhaling the mercury fumes used in the dome's elaborate gilding process.

The northeast bell tower contains St Isaac's heaviest bell, weighing three tonnes.

🔟 Peterhof

An extravagant collection of palaces, fountains and landscaped gardens, Peterhof is located on the shore of the Gulf of Finland. Having originally come across the site in 1705, Peter the Great commissioned the building of a palace here in 1714. He intended the estate to resemble, and indeed rival, that of Versailles in France. The Great Palace (1714–21), originally designed by Jean Baptiste Le Blond, was later transformed during the reign of Elizabeth by Bartolomeo Rastrelli, the architect of the Winter Palace (see p10), who added its distinctive Baroque element.

The Cottage Palace

🚤 An exciting way to travel to or from Peterhof is by hydrofoil. Boats depart from the Gulf of Finland for the city, and leave St Petersburg from Nab. Dvortsovaya, near the beautiful Winter Palace *(see p10)*. The journey across takes less than an hour.

🍽 There are a number of restaurants and cafés scattered around the estate.

• Map G1
• Peterhof, 30 km (19 miles) W of St Petersburg
• 420 0073
• Open Tue–Sun 10am–6pm, closed last Tue of the month
• Fountains operate May–Oct 11am–5pm Mon–Fri, 11am–6pm Sat & Sun
• Hydrofoil: Early Jun–early Oct; every hour from 9:30am–6pm
• Adm: Estate 300 roubles; Palace 500 roubles
• www.peterhof.org

Top 10 Features

1. The Grand Cascade
2. The Throne Room
3. The Imperial Suite
4. The Main Staircase
5. Monplaisir
6. The Hermitage
7. Marly Palace
8. Cottage Palace
9. The Neptune Fountain
10. The Pyramid Fountain

The Grand Cascade
Comprising 37 gilded bronze sculptures, 64 fountains and 142 water jets, the Grand Cascade *(right)* descends from the terraces of the Great Palace, through the estate, and finally out into the gulf.

The Throne Room
This opulent room *(above)*, initially created in Baroque style in 1753 and redesigned by Yuriy Velten in 1770, contains portraits of Russia's imperial family.

The Imperial Suite
Located in the palace's east wing, the suite contains Peter's Oak Study – a rare example of Le Blond's original design. The oak panels date from 1716–21.

The Great Palace

The Main Staircase
With its allegorical sculpture of Elizabeth in the guise of Spring, Rastrelli's creation *(below)* is a stately sight.

From 1944–90, the town of Peterhof was known as Petrodvorets. It is still referred to as such by some of the locals.

5 Monplaisir
Monplaisir ("my pleasure" in French), with its beautiful gardens and flowerbeds, was Peter's favourite palace. He often held parties here, during which his guests were subjected to a punishing regime of drinking. While not as lavish as the Great Palace, the interiors are still impressive.

6 The Hermitage
This pavilion (1721–5) *(above)*, once used as a private dining venue by the tsar and his friends, stands aloof on the shores of the gulf. To highlight the need for solitude, the building is surrounded by a moat.

7 Marly Palace
The palace, built for the tsar's guests, is set in a formal garden with sculptures, fountains and Niccolo Michetti's Golden Hill Cascade. A few of the rooms *(below)* are open to the public.

8 Cottage Palace
More imposing than its name suggests, this Neo-Gothic house (1826–9), set in the gardens of Alexandria Park, was built for Nicholas I and his wife, who had bourgeois tastes and wanted a domestic environment.

9 The Neptune Fountain
The Neptune Fountain's Baroque sculpture *(left)* was originally erected in Nuremberg, Germany, in 1658. It was sold to Paul II in 1782 by local authorities as a lack of water in the town had rendered it unusable.

Nazi Occupation
Peterhof was occupied for three years during World War II by Nazi soldiers laying siege to the city. They burnt the Great Palace and extensively damaged several of the structures. The estate was gradually restored after the war.

The Pyramid Fountain 10
The fountain *(right)*, dating from 1721, is formed by 550 jets rising in seven tiers. Commemorating the Russian victory over Sweden in 1709, it was badly damaged by Nazi bombs during WWII.

🔟 Tsarskoe Selo

The magnificent palaces and gardens at Tsarskoe Selo were established as a country retreat by Catherine I, wife of Peter the Great. However, it was Tsarina Elizabeth who began extensive work on the estate by commissioning the lavish Catherine Palace. The imperial palace was initially created by Rastrelli, but later redesigned by the Scottish architect, Charles Cameron, at the request of Catherine the Great. The landscaped gardens, created in the late 18th century, were the first of their kind in Russia. Tsarskoe Selo suffered extensive damage during World War II and restoration work continues to this day.

Statue on the exterior

The Grotto

⭐ Avoid visiting Tsarskoe Selo on national holidays *(see p102)* as it can get very crowded at these times.

🍴 The Imperial Palace Restaurant at the Catherine Palace is a convenient place for a snack or a meal.

- Map H2
- 25 km (16 miles) W of St Petersburg
- 465 9424 / 465 2196
- Open 10am–5pm Wed–Mon; closed last Mon of the month
- Train from Vitebsk station to Detskoe Selo, then bus 371 or 382
- Adm: Palace 500 roubles
- http://eng.tzar.ru/

Top 10 Features

1. Amber Room
2. The Grotto
3. The Great Hall
4. The Great Staircase
5. Green Dining Room
6. The Blue Drawing Room
7. The Cavalier's Dining Room
8. Small Enfilade
9. Formal Gardens
10. The Cameron Gallery

Amber Room

Created in Prussia, the room's amber panels were gifted to Peter the Great in 1716. It was looted by Nazi troops during World War II. Restoration work, based on old photos, took place between 1979–2003.

The Grotto

Construction of Rastrelli's Grotto began in 1749, but work on the interior, which consists of over 250,000 shells, was not finished for the next quarter of a century.

The Catherine Palace

The Great Hall

The Great Hall *(below)* located in the Catherine Palace, features mirrors, ornate carvings and a huge ceiling painting, *The Triumph of Russia* (c.1755) by Giuseppe Valeriani.

The Great Staircase

Situated in the centre of the Catherine Palace, this marble staircase, designed by Ippolito Monighetti, was built in 1860. The walls of the landings are adorned with decorative 18th- and 19th-century Oriental porcelain vases and dishes.

Green Dining Room

The pistachio-coloured walls of the room *(above)*, designed by Charles Cameron, are decorated with stucco figures by the Russian Neo-Classical sculptor Ivan Martos.

The Blue Drawing Room

Notable for its unusual wallpaper – blue floral motifs painted on silk – this room contains a portrait of Peter the Great by Ivan Nitkin, dating from 1720.

The Cavalier's Dining Room

Elizabeth's gentlemen-in-waiting dined here. The table is permanently laid in this refined gold and white room *(below)*, designed by Rastrelli.

Small Enfilade

A long, captivating suite of halls, parlours and reception rooms, the Small Enfilade boasts a wide collection of period furniture. It also contains some fine examples of Oriental rugs.

Formal Gardens

These lovely gardens *(left)* are laid out symmetrically, and include finely trimmed trees and hedges, as well as geometrically planned flowerbeds complemented by marble statues.

Ahead of its Time

The Tsarskoe Selo estate is part of the nearby town, Pushkin. This town, originally called Tsarskoe Selo, was renamed in 1937 in honour of Russia's national poet *(see p34)*, who attended school here in 1811–17. Founded in the 19th century, the town boasted the first citywide electrical system in Europe, as well as advanced sewage and water systems. It was also the home of the first radio station (1916) in Russia.

The Cameron Gallery

This Neo-Classical section *(right)* of the Catherine Palace features busts of philosophers and thinkers. It was a favourite of Catherine the Great's, especially during her later years.

The nearby town of Pushkin, to the northeast of the Catherine Palace, is also worth a visit.

TOP 10 Pavlovsk

Pavlovsk, an 18th-century park and palace ensemble, is notable for its atmospheric landscaped grounds, containing temples, pavilions and stone bridges. Catherine the Great gifted the estate to her son, the future Paul I, in 1777 and Pavlovsk (from "Pavel" or Paul) was named in his honour. Architect Charles Cameron was commissioned to begin work on it in 1780, and Paul I's wife, Maria Fyodorovna, was the driving force behind the development of the palace's exhaustive collections. Maria, being infatuated with both Pavlovsk and Europe, travelled with Paul throughout the continent, bringing back many sculptures, paintings and silk sets.

One of the Muses

Paul's Mausoleum

🔗 One of the great pleasures of a trip to Pavlovsk is strolling through its romantic grounds, so be sure to pay a visit when the weather is fit for walking.

🔗 There are good restaurants in the Great Hall of the Pavlovsk Palace.

- Map H2
- 30 km (19 miles) S of St Petersburg
- 452 1536
- Open 10am–5pm Sat–Thu, closed first Mon of every month
- Train from Vitebsk, Kupchino or Moscovskay stations, then bus 370, 383, 383a, 493, K-286, K-299
- Adm: Park 30 roubles; Palace 150 roubles
- www.pavlovsk museum.ru/english

Top 10 Features

1. Pavlovsk Palace
2. The Apollo Colonnade
3. The Muses
4. Temple of Friendship
5. Pil Tower and Bridge
6. Visconti Bridge
7. Cold Baths
8. Cameron's Dairy
9. The Rose Pavilion
10. Paul's Mausoleum

Pavlovsk Palace

This modest palace (1782–6) *(right)* consists of a series of remarkably well-preserved rooms and halls that afford the visitor a revealing glimpse into the lifestyle of Russia's pre-revolutionary nobility.

The Apollo Colonnade

This graceful colonnade *(left)* encircles a copy of the Apollo Belvedere. Following a storm in 1817, a new iron Apollo replaced the bronze original.

The Muses

The nine Muses (1780–98), based on statues in the museums of Rome and Florence, were created in the workshops of the Russian Academy.

Temple of Friendship

This Doric temple (1780) *(right)*, dedicated to Catherine the Great, is the earliest example of Greek forms in Russia.

5 Pil Tower and Bridge
Built by Vincenzo Brenna in 1795, the tower *(below)* at one time contained a spiral staircase, library and lounge. The nearby bridge was added in 1808.

6 Visconti Bridge
The most famous and attractive bridge in the park, the Visconti Bridge *(above)* was designed by Andrey Voronikhin in 1807. Its arch stretches lazily over the river, reflected in the water below to form a graceful oval.

7 Cold Baths
This austere pavilion *(below)* was constructed by Cameron in 1799 as a summer swimming pool. It had an elegant vestibule, paintings, furniture and rich wall upholstery.

8 Cameron's Dairy
Important visitors to the estate were invited to this working dairy, a small building with a thatched roof, to sample simple peasant fare.

10 Paul's Mausoleum
This mausoleum bears the inscription "To my beneficent consort". Despite its name, and although constructed in the form of an ancient Roman temple, it never held Paul I's remains.

9 The Rose Pavilion
The Rose Pavilion *(below)* was designed around the theme of the rose. Maria Fyodorovna often entertained guests in this cottage. Alexander I's victory over Napoleon was celebrated here too.

A Scottish Architect in Russia

Having read Charles Cameron's book about Roman public baths, Catherine the Great invited the architect to Russia to work on the reconstruction of her summer palace at Tsarskoe Selo *(see pp26–7)*. Pleased with his work there, she "lent" him to her son, the then Grand Duke Paul, to work on the Pavlovsk estate.

Following pages **Ceiling detail, St Isaac's Cathedral**

Left **Marchers in St Petersburg during the 1917 Revolution** Right **Pro Yeltsin soldier, 1991 Coup**

🔟 Moments in St Petersburg's Histor

1 Founding of the City
St Petersburg was founded by Peter the Great in 1703 as Russia's "Window to Europe". Constructed on swampland, it was built by thousands of serfs, many of whom perished, their bones laying the city's foundations. It became the capital of Russia in 1712, and remained so until 1918.

2 "Bloody Sunday"
On 9 January 1905, peaceful demonstrators carrying a petition to Nicholas II were gunned down by the army as they marched towards the Winter Palace. Around 1,000 demonstrators perished. The aftermath of the horrifying event led to the 1905 Revolution.

3 1917 Revolution
Following a series of strikes in 1917, the tsar was forced to abdicate, and a provisional

An artistic depiction of Bloody Sunday

Peter the Great, Founder of St Petersburg

government assumed power. This was the signal for exiled revolutionaries, led by Vladimir Lenin, to return to Russia, where they overthrew the fledgling government in October, heralding the start of more than 70 years of Soviet rule.

4 WWII Siege
The 900-day siege of Leningrad, which began in 1941 when Nazi forces encircled the city, plunged its three million inhabitants into a living hell. By the time the siege was finally broken in 1944, around two million people had lost their lives to starvation and bitter winters.

5 1991 Coup
The military coup occurred when hardliners opposed to President Gorbachev's reforms seized power. Supporters of Gorbachev's policies gathered in Palace Square *(see p10)* to protest events. The coup was eventually defeated.

6 Name Changes
Originally founded as St Petersburg, the city's name was changed to the more Russian sounding Petrograd in 1914, then to Leningrad in 1924, after the death of Vladimir Lenin. Its original name was restored following the collapse of the USSR in 1991.

Perestroika *(restructuring)* and glasnost *(openness)* were policies introduced by President Gorbachev in 1985.

7 "Criminal" 1990s

Immediately after the era of *perestroika*, a criminal class sprung up, willing and able to do anything to build up fortunes. During this period, St Petersburg earned the reputation as the "Crime Capital of Russia".

8 Reburial of Nicholas II

After the 1917 Revolution, Nicholas II and his family were executed in Yekaterinburg. In 1998, their remains were reburied in the Cathedral of SS Peter and Paul *(see pp20–21)*.

9 300th Anniversary

St Petersburg's 300th anniversary saw a long-needed renovation of the city. The celebrations were attended by the heads of government from more than 45 countries and lasted for over ten days.

10 Election of Vladimir Putin

A St Petersburg native, Putin came into power as Acting President on New Year's Eve, 1999. A former KGB man, he has overseen the country's economic growth as well as a crackdown on press freedom.

Vladimir Putin

Top 10 St Petersburg Political Figures

1 Peter the Great

Peter the Great, the driving force behind the city, ruled Russia from 1682–1725.

2 Nicholas II

The last tsar of Russia, he was killed by the Bolsheviks following the 1917 Revolution.

3 Rasputin

A peasant mystic whose scandalous lifestyle helped discredit Nicholas II's rule *(see p74)*.

4 Mikhail Bakunin

A revolutionary involved in insurrections all over Europe, generally considered the "father of modern anarchism".

5 Lenin

Leader of the 1917 Revolution and first head of the Soviet Union, Lenin changed Russia forever.

6 Sergey Kirov

A Soviet revolutionary whose assassination marked the beginning of a series of purges in the 1930s.

7 Anatoly Sobchak

St Petersburg's first democratically elected mayor, who took office in 1991.

8 Galina Starovoitova

A politician known for her democratic principles. Assassinated in 1998, her funeral was attended by thousands of mourners.

9 Valentina Matvienko

The governor of the city since 2003, she is a rare female figure in male-dominated Russian politics.

10 Vladimir Putin

Putin became Acting President of the Russian Federation on 31 December 1999, and was elected in May 2000. His second term expires in March 2008.

Left **Alexander Pushkin** Centre **Nobel prize winner Joseph Brodsky** Right **Vladimir Nabokov**

🔟 Writers

Pushkin (1799–1837)

Alexander Pushkin's master-piece is *Evgeniy Onegin* (1825–32), a novel set in verse form. The first writer to explore the rich potential of the Russian language as spoken by the common people, he was killed in a duel.

Gogol (1809–52)

Although born in the Ukraine, a huge amount of Nikolai Gogol's strikingly original work, such as *The Nose* (1835) and *The Overcoat* (1842), is set in St Petersburg.

Statue of Gogol on Nevskiy prospekt

Dostoevsky (1821–81)

The author of some of the world's most profound literature, such as *Crime and Punishment*

(1866), Fyodor Dostoevsky spent much of his life in St Petersburg. It was here in 1849 that he was subjected to a mock execution for "revolutionary activities", the trauma of which influenced his future literary work.

Mandelstam (1891–1938)

The author of symbolic, taut poetry, Osip Mandelstam, in 1933, composed his infamous, untitled poem about Stalin, in which he wrote of the dictator's "fingers as fat as grubs" and "cockroach whiskers". The poem, which ultimately led to his death, became known as the "16-line death sentence".

Kharms (1905–42)

Daniil Kharms wrote some of the strangest and most original Russian literature, which was suppressed by Stalin due to its downright oddness rather than any overt political message. The absurdist writer starved to death in the WWII siege of the city *(see p32)*.

Bely (1880–1934)

Although born in Moscow, Andrey Bely reached the pinnacle of his career with his symbolist masterpiece, *Petersburg* (1913), a chaotic, prophetic novel that has been compared to the works of Irish writer James Joyce.

Fyodor Dostoevsky, Russian author

7 Nabokov (1899–1977)

Best known for *Lolita*, Vladimir Nabokov was born in St Petersburg in 1899, and grew up trilingual, speaking Russian, English and French. His family moved to Europe in 1918 and Nabokov wrote many of his novels in English.

8 Brodsky (1940–96)

Joseph Brodsky, protégé of Akhmatova, won the Nobel Prize for Literature in 1987. He left the USSR in 1972 after his works were attacked by the authorities.

Anna Akhmatova

9 Akhmatova (1889–1966)

Branded a "half-harlot, half-nun" by Soviet authorities in 1946, the poetess Anna Akhmatova wrote *Requiem* (1940), her tragic masterpiece about the terrifying Stalin years, which was banned in the USSR until 1989. Her first husband was killed by the Bolsheviks.

10 Blok (1880–1921)

Central to the "Silver Age" of Russian poetry, Alexander Blok developed complex poetic symbols. His controversial work, *The Twelve*, likens Bolshevik soldiers to Christ's Apostles.

Top 10 Films Set in St Petersburg

1 October (1927)

Sergei Eisenstein's film, an epic depiction of the 1917 Revolution, is a silent black and white masterpiece.

2 The End of St Petersburg (1927)

Another film dedicated to the 1917 Revolution, Pudovkin's film forms part of the director's *Revolutionary Trilogy*.

3 The Irony of Fate (1975)

A romantic comedy that uses as its plot device the extreme similarity of Soviet housing.

4 The Burglar (1986)

A *perestroika* favourite, the film portrays the city's underground rock scene.

5 Brother (1997)

A bleak yet humorous film that depicts the chaos of mid-1990s St Petersburg.

6 Golden Eye (1995)

007 comes to St Petersburg to carry out a daring raid involving the Russian Mafia in this action-packed film.

7 Russian Ark (2002)

The world's first unedited feature film, *Russian Ark* is a 90-minute wander through the Winter Palace *(see p10)*.

8 The Idiot (2003)

A highly successful and popular Russian TV adaptation of Dostoevsky's *The Idiot*. Available on DVD everywhere.

9 The Stroll (2003)

Three young people wander around the city discussing life and love.

10 Garpastum (2003)

Love, war and football take equal billing in this impressive film by Alexsei German Jr.

Left **Decorative cans of caviar** Right *Borscht* – **a staple Russian dish**

Russian Dishes

Borscht
A staple Russian/Ukrainian dish, the St Petersburg *borscht* is a filling beetroot-based soup usually prepared with meat, although vegetarian versions can also be found. A thick *borscht* tastes delicious with *smetana* (sour cream).

Caviar
Russia has two types of caviar. Black caviar is the more expensive of the two, and is roe from sturgeon. The red caviar, cheaper and far more common, is roe taken from salmon.

Pelmeni
Pelmeni are like ravioli, only usually bigger. Served in a clear broth or with *smetana*, they come in various shapes, sizes and prices. Avoid the cheaper versions, which often contain meat of an inferior quality.

Pelmeni

Blinis

Blinis
Blinis are buttery pancakes filled with anything from caviar to jam, and are on sale everywhere, from restaurants and cafés to street kiosks.

Solyanka
The main ingredient of *solyanka* is pickled cucumber with brine. This is cooked, and then meat, fish or, occasionally, mushrooms are added to produce a "tangy" tasting soup.

Schi
This cabbage soup, despite sounding like something that Dickens' orphan heroes would be forced to live on, is actually a delicious, warming dish that should be tried at least once. This combination of meat, herbs and vegetables has been popular for over 1,000 years.

Ukha
Ukha is a very popular fish broth usually prepared with salmon, pike or perch. As a rule, *ukha* should be made with a

minimum of two different types
of fish, and a maximum of four.
It also often contains potatoes,
onions and other vegetables.

8 Kholodets
Despite its extremely un-
appetizing appearance, *kholodets*
is a traditional Ukrainian dish that
is incredibly popular all over
Russia. It is made from meat
picked off a boiling bone (traditionally pigs' trotters). As the
meat cools, the gravy around it
forms a kind of jelly. It is served
with mustard or horseradish.

9 Okroshka
Okroshka is another Russian
cold soup which contains an
unlikely combination of ingredi-
ents – cucumber, spring onion,
boiled eggs, ham and *kvas (see
sidebar)*. It is a refreshing summer soup found everywhere in
Russia. Many families have their
own recipes.

Vareniki with potatoes

10 Vareniki
Usually served as dessert,
vareniki are boiled dumplings and
are similar to *pelmeni*. They can
be filled with potato and mush-
room and accompanied with
smetana, or eaten with sweeter
fillings such as cherry or curd. An
excellent option for vegetarians
in Russia, *vareniki* are lighter
than *pelmeni*.

Top 10 Drinks

1 Vodka
The national drink, its
name is derived from *voda*,
the Russian word for water.

2 Kefir
Kefir is an extremely nutri-
tious, fermented milk drink
that originated in the Northern
Caucasus mountains.

3 Ryazhenka
A sweet-tasting, fermen-
ted, baked milk drink with
many health benefits.

4 Local Beer
Tinkoff, Baltica, Botchkarev
and Nevskoe are local lagers
with varying strengths.

5 Kvas
A slightly alcoholic (less
than 1%) drink made from
fermented rye and barley.

6 "Soviet Champagne"
"Soviet", though the USSR
hasn't existed for years;
"champagne" in defiance of
international rulings that make
it illegal to call sparkling wine
"champagne" unless it comes
from that region of France.

7 Mors
A traditional Russian juice
drink, Mors is a red, vitamin-
packed mixture of water and
cranberry or lingberry juice.

8 Samogon
Local equivalent of hooch
or moonshine – you may be
offered some of this if you are
invited to a country cottage.

9 Tea
Tea was introduced to
Russia in 1600. It is sometimes drunk with a lemon or
fruit preserve, but very rarely
with milk.

10 Georgian Wine
A very popular wine in
Russia, supplies are currently
erratic due to the country's
dispute with Georgia.

Left **St Petersburg Opera** Centre *The Sleeping Beauty* ballet performance Right **A local casino**

🔟 Entertainment

1 Ballet
Towards the end of the 17th century, Peter the Great invited foreign ballet instructors to teach in Russia. Since then, the art form has flourished in the country, which has produced stars like Anna Pavlova and Nureyev.

2 Opera
The first opera was performed in Russia in 1731, while the first was written in Russian in 1755. The 19th century produced opera greats such as Mikhail Glinka and Pyotr Tchaikovsky.

3 Theatre
Russian speakers as well as theatre enthusiasts will find the performances a rewarding experience. Russia is the home of Stanislavsky (who pioneered the method acting approach) and playwrights such as Chekhov.

4 Classical Music
Russia's outstanding composers include Prokofiev, Stravinsky and Dmitriy

Alexandriinskiy Theatre

Great Hall of the Philharmonia

Shostakovich. The latter's "Seventh Symphony" was performed in 1942 during the siege of the city, speakers turned defiantly towards Nazi lines.

5 Football
Football is experiencing a boom in Russia. St Petersburg's extremely popular local team, Zenit, currently play at the Petrovskiy Stadium *(see p93)*.

6 Nightclubs
St Petersburg is second only to Moscow for its nightlife. The city has clubs for every taste, from the arty Tunnel *(see p93)* to the odd phenomena of Russian reggae at Jambala *(see p87)*.

7 Cinema
Although Soviet film was respected globally, the industry suffered in post-*perestroika*

In Russia, most ballet, opera, classical music and evening theatre performances begin at 7pm.

Russia. However, recent years have seen a real revival. There are a few cinemas along Nevskiy prospekt, such as Aurora Cinema at 60 and Crystal Palace at 72. The one at 57 is a good place to catch recent Russian releases.

8 Live Rock Music
St Petersburg was the birth-place of some of Russia's finest *perestroika*-era rock groups, including the enigmatic Kino. Venues like Fish Fabrique (see p64) and Griboedov (see p99) continue to host exciting new groups.

9 Wandering through "Piter"
St Petersburg, or "Piter", is a city made for walking: from a relaxed stroll up Nevskiy prospekt or a wander along the city's canals to an all-night White Night hike, the city's skyline is always impressive (see pp6–7).

10 Casinos
Russians have long been famed for their love affair with gambling. However, a new law has been passed that will see all casinos banished to four special zones in the city by the middle of 2009. Head to the Astoria (see p71) to try your luck.

The cinema at 57 Nevskiy prospekt

Top 10 Venues for Ballet, Opera, Theatre and Classical Music

1 Mariinskiy Theatre
One of Russia's most famous venues for ballet and opera (see pp16–17).

2 Mussorgsky Opera and Ballet Theatre
Daily performances of opera and ballet. ⊗ Map N3 • Ploshchad Iskusstv • 595 4284

3 Rimsky-Korsakov Conservatory
An opera, ballet and classical music venue (see p74).

4 October Concert Hall
Daily matinees and evening shows of concerts. ⊗ Map F4 • Ligovskiy prospekt 6 • 275 1273

5 St Petersburg Opera
Performances of less common works of opera, including 18th-century chamber operas. ⊗ Map B4 • Galernaya ulitsa 33 • 312 3982

6 Dom Kochnevoy
A classical music venue on the bank of the Fontanka river. ⊗ Map P4 • Nab. reki Fontanki • 310 2987

7 Alexandriinsky Theatre
Chekhov to modern-day playwrights. ⊗ Map N4 • Pl Ostrovskogo 2 • 710 4103

8 Great Hall of the Philharmonia
A great place for classical music. ⊗ Map N3 • Mikhaylovskiy ulitsa 2 • 710 4275

9 Small Hall of the Philharmonia
A 19th-century concert hall. ⊗ Map N3 • Nevskiy prospekt 30 • 571 8333

10 Academic Capella
A historic venue for classical concerts. ⊗ Map M2 • Nab. reki Moyki 20 • 314 1058

Left **Russian Museum** Centre **Mammoth displays, Zoological Museum** Right **Railway Museum**

🔟 Museums

1 The Hermitage

A treasure trove of master-pieces, an architectural wonder, a symbol of the city's stubborn resistance during WWII – the Hermitage is all this and more. This vast collection features works by Michelangelo, Picasso and Rubens *(see pp10–13)*.

2 Russian Museum

Containing a wide range of works and styles, from the jarring avant-gardism of Kazimir Malevich to the massive canvases of Karl Bryullov, this museum boasts one of the world's best collections of Russian art *(see pp18–19)*.

18th-century crystal vase, Stieglitz Museum

3 Kunstkammer

The Kunstkammer was the city's first museum, built bet-ween 1718–34 to house Peter the Great's collection of anato-mical curiosities. The museum's bizarre first exhibition included

The Hermitage

live dwarves, giants and two-headed animals. Peter was so eager to share his hobby with the world that he instructed the museum to offer free *salo* (pig fat) and vodka to boost attend-ance. Some of the original exhi-bits are still on display *(see p83)*.

4 Stieglitz Museum

Taking its name from Baron Aleksandr Stieglitz, a wealthy industrialist who started an art collection to aid the education of local stu-dents in 1876, the museum contains exhaustive displays of glassware and ceramics. The stunning, medieval-style Terem Room is a highlight *(see p95)*.

5 Pushkin House-Museum

Pushkin *(see p34)* enjoys in Russia fame akin to that of Shakespeare in the UK. This museum contains many of the writer's personal effects, giving an insight into his life. ◈ *Map M2* • *Nab. reki Moyki 12* • *571 3531* • *Open 10:30am–5pm daily* • *Adm*

6 Artillery Museum

Military enthusiasts will find a visit to this museum, housed in the outer fortifications of the Peter and Paul Fortress *(see pp20–21)*, particularly rewarding. Used at one time as an arsenal, the museum contains more than 600 exhibits, ranging from tanks

 Most museums stop selling tickets an hour before closing time.

The Peter and Paul Fortress, home to the Artillery Museum

and rocket launchers to an armoured car in which Lenin rode during the heady days of the 1917 Revolution *(see p89)*.

Zoological Museum

7 The Zoological Museum has one of the world's best collections of mammoths, including a 44,000-year-old specimen dug up in Siberia in 1902. Dating from 1826, the museum contains over 1.5 million specimens, including stuffed bears, wolves and giant crabs *(see p84)*.

Dostoevsky House Museum

8 This evocative museum was the final home of novelist Fyodor Dostoevsky *(see p34)*. By exhibiting the writer's personal effects, this museum explores the human side to the genius's character. ⊗ *Map E5* • *Kuznechnyy perulok 5/2* • *571 4031* • *Open 11am–6pm Tue–Sun* • *Adm*

Nabokov Museum

9 This museum is housed in the Style-Moderne mansion where the world-famous writer Vladimir Nabokov *(see p35)* grew up. After the 1917 Revolution, the Nabokov family's property was confiscated. As a result, almost all the exhibits have come from friends and relatives of the family, who donated such items as the young Nabokov's books and the family's personal items. ⊗ *Map J4* • *Bolshaya Morskaya 47* • *315 4713* • *Open 11am–6pm Tue–Fri, noon–5pm Sat–Sun* • *Adm* • *http://www.nabokovmuseum.org/en/*

Railway Museum

10 This museum boasts comprehensive displays on the history of the Russian railway system from its inauguration in 1813. Exhibits include a model of a formidable-looking armoured train used to transport Bolshevik revolutionaries in 1917 *(see p74)*.

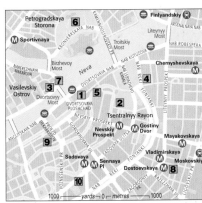

Left **Idiot** Centre **The upmarket Davidov** Right **Blinnyy Domik**

🔟 Russian Restaurants

1 Idiot
When Idiot opened in the early 1990s, its vegetarian menu proved an immediate hit with the local expat community. It serves meat-free versions of Russian food, from *borscht* to *pelmeni* (see p70).

2 Russian Kitsch
With its ironic images of Soviet leaders and menus bound in the ideological works of Lenin, Russian Kitsch reduces the one-time Soviet "threat" to a surreal dining experience. The food, an eclectic mix of Russian, European and Asian, is good too (see p86).

Literary Café's menu card

3 Literary Café
Centrally located, this café is famous as the place where the national poet Pushkin (see p34) met his double before setting off for the duel in which he would lose his life. The café, it must be said, has made the most of this historical hook, and its food, while perfectly edible, is not as memorable as the ideal setting.
⊛ Map L3 • Nevskiy prospekt 18 • 312 6057 • Open 10am–midnight • Adm

4 Blinnyy Domik
Dedicated to that staple of the Russian diet, the pancake, Blinnyy Domik is a cosy restaurant offering over thirty different fillings ranging from mushrooms to caviar. Its generous portions and tasty offerings have made it one of the city's most popular establishments. It also serves *medovukha*, an alcoholic, honey-based drink (see p63).

5 Caviar Bar
The Caviar Bar, located within in the sumptuous Grand Hotel Europe (see p112), is, if your budget will stretch, one of the best places in St Petersburg to sample black caviar. Also on offer is a fine range of traditional Russian food along with an exhaustive selection of vodkas, including some flavoured varieties.
⊛ Map N3 • Mikhalyovskaya ulitsa 1/7 • 329 6651 • Open 5:30pm–midnight • Adm

6 Road to Communism
Packed with reminders of Russia's Soviet past, the Road to Communism is adorned with posters and flags extolling the

Road to Communism's interiors

...tues of the communist ...ystem. The menu features tradi-...onal Russian fare, from ...ancakes to a large selection of ...odka. The waitresses are ...essed in traditional Soviet ...utfits, and there is a big screen ...aturing Soviet pop. ◎ *Map E4 •* ...itsa Zhukovskogo 45 • 579 8902 • Open ...oon–midnight • Adm*

Na Zdorovie!
Serving fresh, delicious ...ussian food at reasonable ...ices, Na Zdorovie! ("To your ...ealth!") needs no gimmicks to ...ecommend it. The kind of place ...here you feel obliged to down ...shot of vodka or two, this res-...urant is somewhat out of the ...ay, but worth a visit if you ...e in the area. The pancakes ...e particularly tasty here. ...here is live gypsy and ...ussian folk music ...the evenings. ...*Map B1 • Bolshoy ...rospekt 13/4 • 232 ...039 • Open noon– ...pm • Adm (free Thu)*

Davidov
Located in the luxurious ...storia Hotel, Davidov offers top-...uality international and Russian ...uisine, including imaginative ...lack and red caviar dishes to ...val those found at the ...rand Hotel Europe ...ee p70).*

Russian Empire
Containing three ...eparate dining ...ooms, and set in ...hat was once a part ...f the Stroganov ...alace *(see p9),* ...ussian Empire is a ...hrowback to the time ...f the tsars. Featuring ...ognac from 1812,

Russian Empire's extravagant setting

and delicious food served on genuine Versace porcelain plates, this restaurant offers perhaps the most extravagant dining experience in the whole of Russia *(see p63).*

Palkin
Founded in 1785, Palkin has long been the haunt of some of the city's finest writers, including Dostoevsky and Gogol *(see p34).* Superb, traditional "imperial Russia" cuisine shares the menu with more exotic creations, such as lobsters' necks with black caviar and avocado. Fashionable Palkin also houses a permanent display of local art. ◎ *Map P4 • Nevskiy prospekt 47 • 703 5371 • Open noon–last guest • www.palkin.ru • Adm*

Russian Empire's cognac collection

A variety of *Matryoshka* dolls

Souvenirs

1 Samovar

The samovar is traditionally used to boil water for tea. Made of brass or copper, and warmed by coals contained in the central tube, the vessel was designed in the 18th century. The word is a combination of *"samo"*, meaning "itself", and *"varit"*, meaning "to boil". A permit is required to export a samovar made before 1945.

2 Matryoshka Dolls

Consisting of a series of carved dolls, each one smaller than the next, *matryoshka* dolls are on sale all over the city and come in a variety of styles. The traditional ones are the prettiest, but those painted as Russian, Soviet and world leaders are also very popular.

A samovar

3 Soviet Memorabilia

While authentic Soviet memorabilia is difficult to find, with factories turning out modern reproductions to meet the booming tourist demand, there are some fine, original Lenin statues on sale at the Souvenir Market near the Church on Spilled Blood. Notes, coins and badges commemorating achievements of the communist system are usually genuine.

4 Gzhel Porcelain

Gzhel porcelain has been produced in Gzhel, an area not far from Moscow, since the middle of the 18th century. The distinctive blue and white patterned ceramics are extremely popular. The Gzhel style is also used in traditional Russian art.

5 Palekh Box

These bright hand-painted boxes were originated in the 18th century in the village of Palekh. Featuring scenes from Russian fairytales, battle scenes or copies of works of art, these boxes range from expensive masterpieces made of paper-mache to cheaper, assembly line-produced ones.

6 Caviar

Black or red caviar makes a great gift. Spread thinly on bread, its distinctive taste is not easily forgotten. It is best to buy caviar in large supermarkets, after carefully checking the expiry date.

Dolls at the Souvenir Market

Chocolate from Krupskaya Fabrika at Ulitsa Vosstaniya 15, semi-precious stones and Lomonosov porcelain make good gifts

7 Vodka

The range of vodka on offer here, from cheap rot-gut to grandly packaged brands, is vast. Stolichnaya and Gzelhka are long-established brands and anything over 200 roubles is almost certain to be safe. Always buy from a supermarket.

A chess set

8 Chess Sets

Russia has long been famed for its chess (*shakhmaty*) and chess sets are available in a variety of styles. These range from the more modest options costing around 500 roubles to handmade sets that can go for up to 2,500 roubles and higher.

9 Russian Music

From choral church music and the *perestroika*-era rock of Kino to the modern day sounds of Leningrad, CDs of Russian music make excellent souvenirs. The best shops are on and near Nevskiy prospekt. Prices usually range from 100 to 300 roubles.

10 DVDs

The streets are full of pirate DVDs of Hollywood hits at rock-bottom prices. The government, under pressure from the WTO, has begun battling against the pirates. As a result, official, great-value versions of films have begun to appear, usually priced from 100 roubles upwards.

Top 10 Customs & Superstitions

1 Empty buckets

A woman carrying an empty bucket is said to be a bad omen.

2 Itchy noses

If your nose itches, you will drink a lot that evening – and there's nothing you can do but accept the fact.

3 Single people at the corners of tables

Single people, at least those who hope one day to wed, should never sit at the corners of tables.

4 Letting cats into new flats first

When moving into a new flat, Russians let cats (preferably black) into the flat first to "chase away the bad luck".

5 Even numbers of flowers

Even numbers of flowers are associated with funerals. Flowers should always be given in odd numbers.

6 Whistling inside

Whistling inside is frowned upon as it will "chase away the money"!

7 Don't give knives as presents

Knives, symbolizing death, are presented as gifts only to one's enemies.

8 Black cat crossing the path

A black cat crossing your path is considered an ill omen.

9 Don't show "wounds"

Using your body to depict wounds or deformities is to tempt fate.

10 Knocking on tables

The Russians knock on wood (usually tables), rather than simply touch it, to avoid bad luck.

Left **Families visiting the Dolphinarium** Centre **Chocolate Museum** Right **A sign for a local zoo**

🔟 Children's Attractions

1 Circus
Russia's oldest circus, which has some of the country's best performers, is a fun place to visit. 🅂 *Map P3 • Nab. reki Fontanki 3 • 314 8478 • Shows 3pm, 7pm • Adm*

2 Naval Museum
This museum contains a superb diorama of the storming of the Winter Palace during the 1917 Revolution. The exterior features an impressive sculpture of Neptune, the sea god *(see p84)*.

3 Boat Ride
In the summer months, a boat ride along the waterways *(see pp54–5)* is an excellent way to see the city. Children will enjoy being on the water, while adults can use the time to take in the magnificent architecture of the "Venice of the North". Boats collect passengers at many locations across the city.

A sculpture outside the Circus

4 Dolphinarium
The dolphin shows are fun for all the family. When booking a ticket, try to get a place on the top seats – from here, the underwater action is clearly visible, and you also avoid getting soaked.
🅂 *Konstantinovsky prospekt 19 • 235 4631 • Shows 3pm, 6pm Wed–Sun • Adm; under 5s free*

5 Troika (Sleigh) ride at Shuvalovka
A winter ride through the thick snow on a *troika*, a traditional Russian sleigh led by horses, is an unforgettable experience. Rides can be booked at Shuvalovka, a replica Russian village that also offers a range of facilities, including a traditional Russian *banya* (sauna). Take a Peterhof bus from Avtovo metro station, and ask the driver to stop at Shuvalovka.
🅂 *Sankt Petersburgskoe Shosse 111 • 450 5393 • Call for timings • Adm • www.russian-village.ru*

Boat rides along the Moyka river

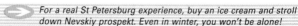

For a real St Petersburg experience, buy an ice cream and stroll down Nevskiy prospekt. Even in winter, you won't be alone!

Puppet Theatre

6 While the language barrier may make a lot of children's entertainment inaccessible, a performance at a puppet theatre poses no problems. The best is the Bolshoi Puppet Theatre, where shows are based around Russian fairy tales. ◙ *Map E3 • Ulitsa Nekrasova 10 • 273 6672 Shows 3pm, 7pm • Adm*

The entrance to the Puppet Theatre

Oceanarium

7 St Petersburg's Oceanarium was opened in 2006, and was the very first in Russia. Featuring over 4,500 species of fish, including 25 sharks, and numerous squids, it makes for a great family day out. There is an oddly captivating shark feeding show every day at 7pm. The souvenir shop has a large selection of mementoes, including decorative shells. ◙ *Map E5 • Ulitsa Marata 8 448 0077 • Open 10am–9pm • Adm www.planeta-neptun.ru*

Chocolate Museum

8 Not a museum as such, the Chocolate Museum is a shop displaying and selling all manner of items crafted from chocolate. From lions and chessboards, to Lenin and the latest pop stars, the Chocolate Museum is worth half an hour of anyone's time, especially people with children. ◙ *Map L3 • Nevskiy prospekt 17 • 315 1348 • Open 10am–7pm*

Zoo

9 One of the world's northern-most zoos, the Leningrad Zoo (it retains the city's Soviet-era name) was opened in 1865. It contains numerous attractions, from polar bears to a monkey-inhabited island. The territory is surprisingly small and some of the animals are kept in cramped conditions. ◙ *Map C2 • Alexandrovskiy Park • 232 8260 • Open 10am–8pm • Adm • www.spbzoo.ru*

Children's Music Theatre

10 The musical theatre is another form of entertainment where the language barrier is easily overcome. Featuring performances of fairy tales, both Russian and foreign, and a musical version of Tolkien's *The Hobbit*, the theatre's wonderful singers and scenery make this a real treat for adults as well as children. ◙ *Map P4 • Ulitsa Rubinshteyna 13 • 712 5135 • Call for timings • Adm • www.zazerkal.spb.ru*

Left **Ploshchad Vosstaniya station** Centre **Dibenko station** Right **Narvskaya station**

🔟 Metro Highlights

1 Avtovo Station

The Avtovo station, like the vast majority of metro stations in Russia, was constructed during the Soviet period. It opened in 1955 and was intended to act as one of many "Palaces for the People". Complete with chandeliers and marble columns, this station reveals a fascinating part of the city's history. The station's *Woman with Child* mosaic is topped with the words "Peace to the World".

2 Ploshchad Vosstaniya Station

While the interior of the Ploshchad Vosstaniya station is highly ornate, the distinguished exterior – a curious circular structure topped with a steeple – has a crumbling beauty. The station was part of the 1955 Line One construction and is dedicated to the 1917 Revolution. Today the building is the subject of ongoing restoration work, and is, at times, obscured by scaffolding and advertising billboards.

Avtovo station

3 Kirovsky Zavod Station

Kirovsky Zavod station (1955), which means "Kirov Factory station", is named after a nearby factory. Although the station's elegant design, with its marble columns and wide platform, was intended to pay homage to the achievements of Soviet industry, the building resembles an ancient Greek temple – the structure is supported by huge columns.

4 Pushkinskaya Station

Named after Pushkin, Russia's national poet *(see p34)*, this station is one of the most beautiful in St Petersburg. A statue of a pensive Pushkin forms the centrepiece of the station, which is a masterpiece of architectural design. Pushkinskaya station was opened in 1956, later than the other stations on Line One, due to problems with tunneling.

5 Frunzenskaya Station

Named in honour of the Bolshevik leader Mikhail Frunze, Frunzenskaya metro station was opened in 1961 as part of St Petersburg's Line Two project. Its central feature is a large monument depicting Frunze with his revolutionary comrades. In comparison with many other stations in the city, Frunzenskaya has a relatively simple design, notable for its absence of ornate chandeliers and marble columns.

 Due to the difficulties of tunneling around the Neva Delta, the St Petersburg metro is the deepest in the world.

Kirovsky Zavod station

Sportivnaya Station
Operational since 1997, this station is one of the newest in St Petersburg. It is located close to Petrovskiy Stadium *(see p93)*, although trains do not stop here before, during or immediately after matches. The station's interior includes two large murals, and an ode to sport that includes the line *"O' Sport, you are Joy!"*.

Ploshchad Alexandra Nevskogo Station
Ploshchad Alexandra Nevskogo is notable for the colourful mural immediately inside the entrance, which depicts Russia's defeat of Swedish invaders in the 13th century. Opened in 1985, this was St Petersburg's first station on the Pravoberezhnaya (right bank) Line.

Dibenko Station
When compared to earlier stations, Dibenko, which opened in 1987, is rather austere in design. Located at a distance from St Petersburg's centre, this is one of the last stations to be opened by Soviet authorities before the collapse of the USSR.

Baltiskaya Station
Another Line One metro station dating from 1955, Baltiskaya Station features a large image of Baltic socialist revolutionaries from Latvia, Estonia and Lithuania, hoisting the red flag of socialism aloft in victory. Its exterior is a massive Socialist Realism construction typical of the period.

Narvskaya station
The sculpted figures in the scene inside this station are clearly gazing at someone who is not present – namely Stalin (1878–1953), the dictator whose once-ubiquitous image was removed from all over the USSR following Nikita Krushchev's "secret" denouncement of Stalinism in 1956 *(see p84)*.

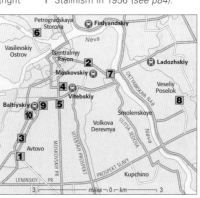

Left **Cruiser _Aurora_** Right **Finland Station**

🔟 Soviet Landmarks

1 Cruiser Aurora
The cruiser _Aurora_ is famed as the ship that fired a blank shot to signal the storming of the Winter Palace, which then began the 1917 Revolution. Today it is open to the public, and the famous gun, along with the crew's quarters, can be viewed _(see p90)._

2 Siege Plaque
This plaque was put up during the darkest days of the Siege of Leningrad _(see p32)_ to warn citizens that the side of the road on which it sat was the most dangerous during an artillery attack. It is a stark reminder of the horrors of WWII, when millions of the city's citizens starved to death _(see p8)._

3 Victory Monument
Erected in 1975 to mark the 30th anniversary of the end of WWII, the Victory Monument commemorates the victims of the siege – it features granite sculptures of grieving mothers and defiant Soviet soldiers. A Memorial Hall at the complex has exhibits demonstrating life during the siege _(see p97)._

Statue of Lenin

4 Statue of Lenin in Ploshchad Lenina
This statue of Lenin, erected in 1926, portrays him delivering a fiery speech to cheering crowds upon his return from exile in 1917. 🗺 Map E2

5 Lenin's Train
Finland Station was opened in the mid 1960s, and contains Locomotive 293, the train on which Lenin rode when returning from exile to Russia to launch the 1917 Revolution that would bring him to power. Once a requisite sight for any Soviet visitor, this train, exhibited in a glass case on platform 5, attracts far less attention these days _(see p95)._

Heroic partisans during the Siege of Leningrad, Victory Monument

Portrait of Sergey Kirov, Kirov Museum

columns, mosaics and murals. It is as if the USSR never ceased to exist and the Cold war never ended – the stations' walls still proudly bear hammers and sickles, and stirring slogans extolling the achievements of the Soviet system *(see pp50–51)*.

Smolnyy Institute
Built in 1806–8 and housed in a Neo-Classical building, the institute was at one time a school for young noblewomen. However, during the 1917 Revolution it was Lenin's seat of power until March 1918, when the Soviets moved the capital from St Petersburg to Moscow. It is also where Sergey Kirov was murdered *(see p96)*.

Museum of Russian Political History
Lenin gave one of his many inspirational speeches from a balcony at this mansion, which is named after ballerina Matilda Kshesinskaya *(see p90)*. Now a museum, it contains Lenin's office, restored to its Soviet-era state. Fascinating memorabilia from the period of revolutionary struggle is housed upstairs.

Revolution Square
Now known as Trinity Square, Revolution Square was the name given by the Soviets to the site of one of the most brutal scenes of "Bloody Sunday", *(see p32)*. Today, belying its bloody past, the square is a pleasant area *(see p89)*.

Kirov Museum
This museum is located in the one-time flat of Sergey Kirov, a Stalin-era politician. Charismatic Kirov reportedly enjoyed grassroots popularity, leading Stalin to fear him as a rival. Most historians believe that Stalin arranged Kirov's assassination, and then used it as an excuse to launch a series of purges to punish the "guilty" *(see p89)*.

The Metro
Designed as monuments to the working class, the city's pre-*perestroika* metro stations are socialist palaces, complete with chandeliers, marble

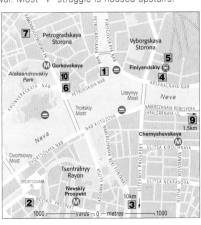

Left **Architectural details, Anichkov Bridge** Right **The Lomonosov Bridge's granite towers**

🔟 Bridges and Waterways

1 Trinity Bridge
Opened in 1903 to commemorate the 200th anniversary of the founding of St Petersburg, Trinity Bridge is one of the most beautiful of the city's 800 bridges. It consists of ten arches and elegant Style-Moderne lamp posts. ◈ Map M1

2 Griboedov Canal
This canal, stretching 5 km (3 miles) through the very centre of the city, is crossed by 21 bridges. It was constructed in 1739 to move cargo from Sennaya ploshchad, and named after the Russian playwright and diplomat, Alexander Griboedov. ◈ Map L5

3 Bridge Passage
Linking the junction of the Griboedov Canal and the Moyka river, the Bridge Passage (1829–31) is a cleverly constructed piece of architecture. Consisting of the Malo-Konyushenny and Theatre bridges, and designed to give the impression of a single bridge, the Bridge Passage contains beautiful metal railings and lamp posts. ◈ Map N1

Bridge Passage

4 Anichkov Bridge
The three-span Anichkov Bridge (1839–41) is noteworthy for its evocative bronze statues of men taming wild horses. Designed by the Russian sculptor Pyotr Klodt, the statues symbolize man's taming of the forces of Mother Nature. When viewed in an anti-clockwise direction, the wild horses seem to steadily become domesticated. ◈ Map P4

Griboedov Canal

5 Lomonosov Bridge
Notable for its curious stone turrets, this bridge is named in honour of the Russian scientist Mikhail Lomonosov (1711–65). Built between 1785 and 1787, the bridge's granite towers were originally used to house its opening mechanism. When the bridge was rebuilt in 1912, the towers, having become a landmark, were left in place. ◈ Map N5

During summer, the bridges on the Neva river are raised to let ships through.

The narrow Bank Bridge

Bank Bridge

Dating from 1825–6, this pleasant pedestrian bridge is less than 2 m (7 ft) wide. It is famous throughout Russia for its four gold-winged griffins, created by Russian sculptor Pavel Sokolov. Seated in eternal contemplation of the waters below, they also serve to hold up the bridge's cables. ✎ Map M4

Egyptian Bridge

This splendid bridge dates from 1955. The current structure replaced the 19th-century original, which collapsed into the Fontanka in 1905 when a large cavalry squadron was passing by. The magnificent sphinxes that adorn the bridge were salvaged from the original bridge, as were the bank supports. ✎ Map B6

Lion Bridge

The two pairs of proud lions on Lion Bridge, a Pavel Sokolov creation, date from 1825–6. This was one of the city's earliest pedestrian suspension bridges, and is today a popular place for romantic meetings. ✎ Map J5

Blagoveshchenskiy Bridge

This elegant bridge, which has also been known as the Nicholas Bridge and the Lieutenant Shmidt Bridge since its construction in 1850, was the first permanent crossing over the Neva river. The bridge retains its original, intricate cast-iron sea horse and trident railings, designed by Aleksandr Bryullov. Offering great views across the Admiralty and Universitet embankments, this is one of the city's most historic bridges, and a local favourite (see p83).

A serene Sphinx on the Egyptian Bridge

Winter Canal

The narrowest waterway in the city, the Winter Canal is, nonetheless, one of its most picturesque. Constructed in 1718–20, this stretch of water is crossed by three bridges, and by the Hermitage's Theatre Foyer. Namechecked in Pushkin's (see p34) "Queen of Spades", the Winter Canal, particularly beautiful on a freezing winter's day, is yet another favourite for romantic trysts. ✎ Map C3

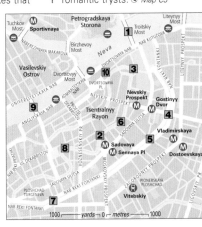

Many of St Petersburg's original bridges were swept away in the great floods of 1842.

AROUND TOWN

ST PETERSBURG'S TOP 10

Left **Statue of Pushkin** Right **Garden at Mikhaylovskiy Castle**

Gostinyy Dvor

DATING FROM THE EARLIEST DAYS *of St Petersburg, this is the city's undisputed commercial, social and cultural centre. The area sums up the paradoxical character of the "Venice of the North", with modern shopping centres standing next to tsarist-era churches and restaurants housed in 18th-century Style-Moderne wonders. From the bustle of Nevskiy prospekt and the Soviet-era Ploshchad Vosstaniya, the vast square commemorating the stirrings of the 1917 Revolution, to the peace and quiet of the secluded Arts Square, Gostinyy Dvor is a microcosm of Russia today and a reminder of the city's rich cultural heritage.*

The Russian Museum's façade

🔟 Sights

1. Church on Spilled Blood
2. Cathedral of Our Lady of Kazan
3. Russian Museum
4. Armenian Church
5. Mikhaylovskiy Castle
6. Sheremetev Palace
7. Arts Square
8. Statue of Pushkin
9. Church of St Catherine
10. Ploshchad Vosstaniya

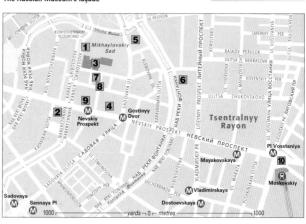

Previous pages **Gostinyy Dvor arcade**

The striking Church on Spilled Blood

Russian Museum

This museum's exhibits explore the history of Russian art from 13th-century icons to modern masterpieces. It contains works by perhaps the greatest of the city's avant-garde painters, Pavel Filonov, an artist little known in the West, but who is reported to be President Putin's favourite. For those with more traditional tastes, the museum also displays calming canvases by landscape painter Ivan Shishkin, another St Petersburg artist *(see pp18–19)*.

Church on Spilled Blood

Despite its typically "Russian" onion domes, this church is something of an anomaly in St Petersburg, a city more famous for its European style architecture. Extensively restored after years of neglect, this church is an example of Russia's Eastern cultural heritage, something that is usually more visible in the capital, Moscow *(see pp14–15)*.

Armenian Church

While today a beautifully decorated building, during the Soviet era and the period immediately after *perestroika*, the Armenian Church lay in ruins, abandoned to the elements. It was handed back to the Armenian community in the mid-1990s. With the help of funds from the vast Armenian diaspora as well as local donations, it was not long before the church was restored to its former glory. The courtyard outside houses a tiny shop selling Armenian snacks.
Ⓝ Map N3 • Nevskiy prospekt 40–42
• 318 4108 • Open 9am–9pm

Cathedral of Our Lady of Kazan

This building was constructed in 1811 solely for housing Russian Orthodoxy's precious, miracle-working icon, Our Lady of Kazan. After the 1917 Revolution, the icon was seized by the atheist Soviet authorities. It resurfaced many years later in New York and is now housed once again in the cathedral. A statue of Field Marshall Kutuzov (1745–1813), a hero in the 1812 war against Napoleon, is just outside the premises. Ⓝ Map M3 • Kazansky ploshchad 2 • 317 5856 • Open 9am–7:30pm

Cathedral of Our Lady of Kazan

Pushkin's African Past

Alexander Pushkin *(see p34)*, whose statue stands in Arts Square, was the great grandchild of an African slave, Abram Hannibal, brought to Russia by Peter the Great. Hannibal gained popularity around the court of the tsar and served as the governor of Tallinn (then known as Reval). Pushkin owed his distinctive curly hair to Hannibal and even began a novel (unfinished) about him.

Mikhaylovskiy Castle

This castle was constructed especially for Paul I in 1797–1801. The tsar's fear of being assassinated led him to surround the castle with moats and draw-bridges, as well as build a secret escape tunnel. Despite all this, the tsar was murdered after just 40 days in his new residence. Today the castle is a branch of the nearby Russian Museum and is used for temporary exhibitions. ✎ *Map P2 • Sadovaya ulitsa 2 • 570 5112 • Open 10am–6pm Wed–Sun, 10am–5pm Mon • Adm*

Sheremetev Palace

This elegant Baroque palace, built in 1750, was originally the residence of the wealthy Sheremetev family. During the Soviet period, one of the attached communal flats was the home of the famous Anna Akhmatova *(see p34)*, who lived here for nearly thirty years. The flat is now a museum dedicated to her life and works. ✎ *Map P3 • Nab. reki Fontanki 34 • 272 2211 • Open 10:30am–6pm Tue–Sun • Adm*

Arts Square

Arts Square is a showpiece for the city's cultural institutions and a patch of green amongst the canals and grand constructions of Gostinyy Dvor. Designed by Carlo Rossi in the early 19th century, it is not far from the Philharmonia Concert Hall, the Russian Museum, the Circus and Mikhaylovskiy Castle. Just opposite is Mikhaylovskiy Garden, and the two areas together form the favourite haunt of lunching office-workers and romantic couples. ✎ *Map N3 • Ploshchad Iskusstv*

Statue of Pushkin

One of many statues of Pushkin, this commanding figure was created by the Russian sculptor, Mikhail Anikushin, in 1957. Dominating Arts Square, Pushkin stands in front of the

Sheremetev Palace

Ploshchad Vosstaniya

Russian Museum, gesturing casually away from it, his pose taken from Ilya Repin's 1911 painting of the poet. Exiled to the Caucasus region of Russia by the tsar, Pushkin was later lauded by the Soviet regime for his perceived anti-bourgeois views – hence the abundance of Pushkin statues and street names around the city. ◈ Map N3 • Ploshchad Iskusstv

Church of St Catherine

Built in 1782, the Church of St Catherine is the oldest Roman Catholic church in Russia. It saw many state funerals in pre-revolutionary Russia, including that of the last king of Poland, who was one of Catherine the Great's many lovers, and those of the heroes of the 1812 war against Napoleon. ◈ Map N3
• Nevskiy prospekt 30 • Open 9am–9pm

Ploshchad Vosstaniya

The vast, imposing Ploshchad Vosstaniya, or Uprising Square, gets its name from the events of February 1917, when a group of Russian soldiers refused to fire upon demonstrators, instead taking up arms on the side of the discontented masses. In 1985, it was the scene of a then-unheralded walkabout by a Soviet leader, when Mikhail Gorbachev went into the masses to discuss the country's problems. ◈ Map E4

A Day Around Nevskiy Prospekt

Morning

Starting around 11am to avoid the morning rush-hour crowds, turn right from the even-numbered side of **Nevskiy prospekt** into the atmospheric nab. Kanala Griboedova. From here, walk down to the **Church on Spilled Blood** at the end of the canal and then walk back up to the exhibition halls of the **Russian Museum** (see p59), where you can feast your eyes upon one of the world's best collections of Russian art. Afterwards, weather permitting, picnic at the nearby **Arts Square**, an oasis of calm in this bustling area. If the weather is bad, then savour some delicious pancakes in the Russian Museum café on the ground floor.

Afternoon

Walk back up nab. Kanala Griboedova and cross Nevskiy prospekt at the traffic lights opposite the metro station. To your right is the **Cathedral of Our Lady of Kazan** (see p59), inspired by St Peter's in Rome. Heading away from the cathedral, take a stroll along Nevskiy prospekt, soaking up the atmosphere and visiting a few souvenir shops. Be sure to stop by at the brooding **Church of St Catherine** and the "Blue Pearl of Nevskiy Prospekt" – the **Armenian Church**. Then head up to the Grand Hotel Europe, and splash out on a caviar and vodka session in the **Caviar Bar** (see p44). If your wallet won't quite stretch to this, make your way to the nearby **Kalinka-Malinka** (see p63) for some tasty traditional Russian food.

Left **Artists' Market** Centre **Souvenir plates** Right **The impressive building that houses Yeliseev's**

Shopping

Gostinyy Dvor Mall
This mall, with over 300 shops, from furniture stores to fashion outlets, is housed in a charming old arcade. Map N4
• Nevskiy prospekt 32 • 710 5408

Dom Knigi
Russia's top bookstore, Dom Knigi has branches all over the country. This branch has a small selection of English books. Map P4 • Nevskiy prospekt 62 • 570 6546

Grand Palace
Expensive boutiques are stocked with European designer labels in this shopping centre. Map N3 • Nevskiy prospekt 44

Passazh
This chic department store sells everything from antiques to cosmetics and is popular with wealthy citizens. Map N3 • Nevskiy prospekt 46

Yeliseev's
The stained glass windows of this famous food store, mentioned in Tolstoy's Anna Karenina, make it look more like a church than a shop. Currently closed for repairs, there are rumours that it may reopen as a clothes shop. Map P3 • Nevskiy prospekt 56

Corinthia Nevskij Palace Shops
Housed in a luxury hotel of the same name, these shops sell expensive items like black caviar. Map E4 • Nevskiy prospekt 57 • 380 2001

Ligovsky Prospekt DVD Shops
These two shops have a vast selection of DVDs, both Russian and foreign, at unbelievably low prices. They also sell computer games and CDs. Map E4
• Ligovsky prospekt 43-45

Artists' Market in front of the Church of St Catherine
If you feel like having your portrait painted or want to buy some original art, then this small, open-air market is where you will find it all. Map M4

Russian Museum Souvenir Shop
Located inside the Russian Museum (see pp18–19), this shop has a fine selection of posters, postcards and books on art. It also sells DVD souvenirs of the museum's exhibits.

Souvenir Market near the Church on Spilled Blood
This open-air market is the place to come to try and track down Soviet memorabilia (see p46). Haggling is welcome, but do not start unless you seriously intend to buy. Map N2

Most shops in St Petersburg open between 9am–10am and close around 7pm.

Sakura's elegant Japanese setting

Price Categories

For a three-course meal	**US$** Under $30
for one including a glass	**US$$** $30–$60
of house wine, all unavoid-	**US$$$** $60–$90
able charges and a	**US$$$$** $90–$120
modest service charge.	**US$$$$$** over $120

Restaurants

1 L'Europa
L'Europa boasts some of the finest food in St Petersburg, along with an extensive wine and cognac list. ✪ *Map N3 • Mikhaylovskaya ulitsa 1/7 • 329 6630 • Closed for lunch on Sun • $$$$$*

2 Shyolk (Silk)
This elegant eatery has a creative fusion menu. DJs play tempo jazz and house at weekends. ✪ *Map M2 • Malaya Konyushennaya ulitsa 4/2 • 571 5078 • $$$$*

3 Russian Empire
The place to come to if you want to dine like the tsars and tsarinas of Imperial Russia. The experience does not come cheap, however. ✪ *Map M3 • Nevskiy prospekt 17 • 571 2409 • $$$$*

4 Sakura
With its delicious Japanese food, Sakura offers a happy medium between chain sushi and the more expensive, elite Japanese restaurants. ✪ *Map M3 • Nab. kanala Griboedova 12 • 315 9474 • $$$*

5 Blinnyy Domik
This popular St Petersburg eatery is known for its cheap and very tasty pancakes with a variety of fillings. ✪ *Map E5 • Kolokolnaya ulitsa 8 • 315 9915 • $*

6 Count Suvoroff
An establishment that prefers to look back to the city's imperial past, Count Suvoroff's dishes are based on those found on 19th-century menus. ✪ *Map N4 • Ulitsa Lomonsova 6 • 315 4328 • $$$$*

7 Kalinka-Malinka
The restaurant, named after a folk song, serves Russian food in a mock-village setting with performances by enthusiastic folk groups. ✪ *Map M3 • Italyanskaya ulitsa 5 • 314 2681 • $$*

8 Fasol (Bean)
Fasol is popular for its superb location right on the corner of the Moyka and tasty, good value lunches. ✪ *Map L4 • Gorokhovaya ulitsa 17 • 571 7454 • $$*

9 Café D'or
Serving *foie gras* and Italian pasta, Café D'or also offers a range of mouth-watering French confectionaries, including honey and jam. ✪ *Map N3 • 44 Nevskiy prospekt • 449 9487 • $$$$*

10 Piter
An unpretentious restaurant with a separate bar catering to football fans, this is a convenient place for a lunchtime snack. ✪ *Map E3 • Ulitsa Mayakovskovo 34 • 275 3023 • $$*

Left **The night scene at Dacha** Centre **Fish Fabrique** Right **Led Lemon's rotating bar**

TOP 10 Clubs

1 Fish Fabrique
A legendary St Petersburg venue, Fish Fabrique puts on live concerts and club nights. ◎ *Map E5 • Ligovskiy prospekt 53 • 764 4857 • Concerts start at 10:30pm–11pm • Adm*

2 Dacha
A popular underground club housed in a very small venue that gets packed and sweaty at weekends. ◎ *Map M4 • Ulitsa Dumskaya 9 • Open 7pm–6am • Adm*

3 Money Honey
One of St Petersburg's oldest clubs, Money Honey plays live rockabilly music every evening and serves cheap beer. ◎ *Map M5 • Ulitsa Sadovaya 28– 30 • 310 0549 • Concerts begin at 10pm • Adm*

4 Stars Only Club
Describing itself as a "restaurant/club", this is a favourite pre-party hangout amongst St Petersburg's disco/Eurodance lovers. ◎ *Map E4 • Nevskiy prospekt 86 • 275 1223 • Open 24 hours • Adm*

5 Cash Bar
An excellently located club that features an eclectic mix of live music. ◎ *Map P3 • Reki Fontanki Nab 23 • 570 6703 • Concerts begin at 9pm • Adm*

6 Led Lemon
This dance-music club has a rotating bar. Entrance is with a club card. ◎ *Map M3 • Nab. Kanala Griboedova 6 • 438 1450 • Free club card: collect between 8pm and 10pm*

7 CCCP
This after-party club is by day a quiet coffee house. Saturday and Sunday mornings see the city's insomniacs gather here to chill out to downtempo dance music. ◎ *Map P4 • Nevskiy prospekt 54 • 310 4929 • Open 24 hours*

8 Seven Sky Bar
This café/club on top of the Grand Palace shopping centre has excellent views and trendy local DJs. ◎ *Map N3 • Italyanskaya ulitsa 15 • 449 9462 • Open noon–2am Sun–Thu, noon–6am Fri–Sat*

9 Stirka
Stirka (the washing) is a launderette/club that features a bar, hookahs and comfortable sofas – it makes for an extremely relaxed clothes-washing experience! ◎ *Map L4 • Ulitsa Kazanskaya 26 • 314 5371 • Open 10am–11pm*

10 Magrib
A Moroccan-themed club that plays a mixture of house and trance, Magrib is very popular with members of St Petersburg's tiny upper-middle class. ◎ *Map E4 • Nevskiy prospekt 84 • 275 7620 • Open 6pm–6am • Adm*

Left **A Beatles poster at Liverpool** Centre **A display at Mollie's Irish Pub** Right **Telegraph**

Top 10 Bars

Telegraph
This British-style pub serves a vast selection of ales and has a large screen that airs sporting events. ◈ *Map P4 • Ulitsa Rubinsteina 3 • 327 7479*

Mollie's Irish Pub
The city's first Irish pub serves a wide range of beers and is popular with the locals. ◈ *Map E5 • Ulitsa Rubinsteina 36 • 570 3768*

Liverpool
This was once a Beatles theme bar, but now plays a wide range of music, including jazz and English rock. A comfortable place to enjoy good food with beer. ◈ *Map E4 • Ulitsa Mayakovskogo 16 • 597 2054*

James Cook
This basement bar is split in two – one half serves cakes and coffee, the other serves alcoholic beverages. The food here is good too, especially the steaks. ◈ *Map M2 • Shedsky pereulok 2 • 312 3200*

Football Bar
This restaurant/bar transforms into football nirvana whenever a big game is on. ◈ *Map P4 • Ulitsa Karavannaya 28 • 314 8468*

Purga
Purga is actually two nightclubs in one, both going by the same name and located right next to each other on the bank of the Fontanka. ◈ *Map P3 • Reki Fontanki Nab 11 • 570 5123 • Adm*

Tinkoff
This bar, named after a brand of high-quality Russian beer, reportedly President Putin's favourite drink, offers a great brewed-on-the-premises selection. ◈ *Map M4 • Kazanskaya ulitsa 7 • 718 5566*

Lobby Bar
This elegant Austrian bar/restaurant, has an excellent location, speedy service, tasty food and an extensive selection of alcoholic drinks. ◈ *Map N3 • Mikhailovskaya ulitsa 1/7 • 329 6622*

The Other Side
A bar that serves an excellent mix of Thai, Chinese and Mexican food, this is fast becoming a St Petersburg favourite. ◈ *Map M2 • Ulitsa Bolshaya Konyushennaya 1 • 312 9554*

Vegas
A large sports bar/casino with a good atmosphere, Vegas also has round-the-clock screenings of sporting events. It is conveniently located too, tucked away just behind Nevskiy prospekt. ◈ *Map P3 • Manezhnaya ploshchad 6 • 710 5050*

Left **The serene Palace Embankment** Right **The Winter Palace at Palace Square**

Palace Embankment

UNLIKE NEARBY GOSTINNY DVOR, *Palace Embankment contains very little in the way of shops and restaurants.* Dominated instead by the symbols of Imperial, pre-revolutionary Russia, this is a particularly elegant area of the city. It showcases the splendour of the Winter Palace, the former residence of the tsars, which is housed in the stunning Hermitage, the colossal St Isaac's Cathedral, as well as the embodiment of imperial strength that is the Bronze Horseman statue. A stroll here highlights the sheer weight of history contained in this city of just under five million people.

🔟 Sights

1. The Hermitage
2. The Admiralty
3. Palace Square
4. The Bronze Horseman
5. St Isaac's Cathedral
6. St Isaac's Square
7. Field of Mars
8. Summer Garden
9. Decembrist's Square
10. Admiralty Gardens

The ceiling of St Isaac's Cathedral

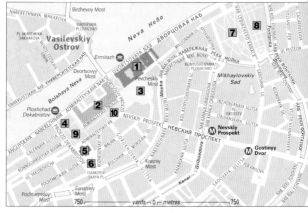

A boat ride is a fascinating way to experience the Palace Embankment and its captivating skyline.

New Hermitage

1 The Hermitage

The famous Hermitage, which consists of five separate buildings, is one of the world's largest museums. Its enormous and breathtaking collection, containing works by Michelangelo, Leonardo da Vinci, Picasso and Rembrandt, is far too large to see in a single day. The New Hermitage is the only purpose-built museum within the complex *(see pp10–13)*.

2 The Admiralty

Immediately after founding St Petersburg, Peter the Great set about building a navy powerful enough to repel any attack on the city and expand Russia's regional ambitions. The Admiralty, built between 1704–11, was originally the shipyard where Russia's first battle-ships were produced. From 1806–23, the Admiralty was rebuilt by the architect Andrey Zakharov, who decorated its 407-m (1,335-ft) wide façade with potent symbols of Russia's now-powerful fleet. Highlights of the building include the Neo-Classical gate tower and the gilded cupola with its 230-ft (70-m) high spire. ✆ *Map K3 • Admiralteyskaya nab. 2 • Closed to public*

3 Palace Square

The city is famed for its wide open spaces, vast squares and never-ending embankments. The gigantic Palace Square perfectly encapsulates the sense of overwhelming expansivenesses one gets when walking the city's streets. Entering the square for the first time is a sensory overload – the eyes are simply unable to process so much at once. Flanked by the Hermitage and the 19th-century General Staff Building, Palace Square has witnessed many historical events over the years, such as the massacre of "Bloody Sunday" *(see p32)*. Before the Revolution, the square was the setting for military parades, often led by the tsar on horseback. It is still a favourite venue for political meetings and public events like rock concerts *(see p10)*.

PETRO
CATHARINA

The Bronze Horseman

4 The Bronze Horseman

This magnificent statue, created by French architect, Etienne Falconet, was unveiled in 1782. Portraying Peter the Great *(see p32)* astride a horse, the bronze sculpture was commissioned by Catherine the Great as a tribute to the founder of the city. A serpent, the symbol of betrayal, is crushed beneath the horse's hooves. The statue was also the subject of an eponymous poem by Pushkin *(see p32)*. ✆ *Map J3*

Eternal Flame, Field of Mars

5 St Isaac's Cathedral

St Isaac's Cathedral, a captivating edifice silhouetted against the St Petersburg sky, stands at the edge of St Isaac's Square. The church's interior is lavishly decorated with marble and other semi-precious stones, and the upper sections of the exterior are adorned with masterfully sculpted figures of saints and angels *(see pp22–3)*.

6 St Isaac's Square

St Isaac's Square was used as a marketplace in the 19th century. It is surrounded by a great number of St Petersburg's most famous buildings and monuments, including the striking St Isaac's Cathedral, the Astoria Hotel *(see p112)* and the Mariinskiy Palace, which houses the St Petersburg City Hall. Also at the square is Pyotr Klodt's statue of Nicholas I, who took Russia into the Crimean War. The reliefs on the pedestal depict events from his 30-year reign. St Isaac's Square features in Gogol's *(see p34)* famous short story, "The Overcoat". ◎ *Map K4* • *Issakievskaya ploshchad*

A Cancelled Celebration

The Astoria Hotel on St Isaac's Square was where Hitler planned to hold a celebratory dinner after the fall of Leningrad. The dictator, so sure he would conquer the city, had already printed invitations and set a date – 9 August 1942. However, Nazi forces were repelled, and the event never took place. An original invitation is framed in the lobby of the Astoria.

7 Field of Mars

This area, appropriately named after the Roman God of War, was used in the 19th century for military manoeuvres and parades. Like much of the city, it was reclaimed from swampland and extensively drained, earning it the nickname, "Sahara of St Petersburg". It contains the Eternal Flame monument (1957), dedicated to those who perished during the 1917 Revolution *(see p32)*, as well as the *Monument to Revolutionary Fighters* (1917–19), by Lev Rudnev. This is a popular spot with locals during spring. ◎ *Map N1* • *Marsovo Pole*

8 Summer Garden

This garden was originally the pet project of Peter the Great *(see p32)*, who spared no expense to create a botanical wonderland, complete with imported trees and plants. However, Peter's Summer Garden was destroyed in a flood in 1777, and the English-style garden that exists today was commissioned by Catherine the Great. It features a splendid bronze statue of Ivan Krylov, the Russian 19th-century writer of fables, sculpted by Pyotr Klodt in 1854. ◎ *Map N1* • *Letniy sad* • *Open Nov–Apr 10am–6pm, May–Oct 10am–10pm*

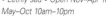

9 Decembrist's Square

This square was the site of an attempted coup by officers of the Russian army who, on 14 December 1825, attempted to seize power during the inauguration of Nicholas I. The rebel forces were quickly suppressed, but it would not be the last time that the new tsar would have to face a challenge to his throne. The square was originally named Senate Square, but was renamed in 1925 to commemorate the 100-year anniversary of the event. ✆ Map K3 • Ploshchad Dekabristov

10 Admiralty Gardens

In winter, the Admiralty Gardens are transformed into a winter wonderland, with mounds of snow filling the pretty ornamental fountain. In summer they are full of relaxing office-workers, students and chess players. The gardens look directly onto the Admiralty (see p67), and are full of busts of famous Russian composers and writers, including the ubiquitous Gogol (see p34), and the 19th-century composer, Mikhail Glinka. ✆ Map K3 • Alexsandrovskiy sad

Admiralty Gardens

A Day of Imperial Wonders

Morning

🕐 Turn off the even-numbered side of Nevskiy prospekt and walk down Bolshaya Morskaya ulitsa, sticking to the left, and an unforgettable view of the **Hermitage** and **Palace Square** (see p67) will open up in front of you. Stroll through the vastness of the square, examining the colossal, freestanding **Alexander Column** (see p11) as you do so. Before entering the Hermitage, wander over to the **Atlantes** (see p11) and the **Winter Canal** (see p55). It is impossible to see every-thing the Hermitage has to offer in one visit, and so, take a break and have lunch at the museum café. If the weather is good, have a picnic in the nearby **Summer Garden** or **Field of Mars**.

Afternoon

After lunch, head away from the river, crossing Palace Square again on your way towards **St Isaac's Square**. Pass through the **Admiralty Gardens** to look at busts of Russian composers and writers, and pay a visit to the **Bronze Horseman** (see p67), a local land-mark. The gardens are a popular spot for taking wedding photographs. Turn away from the embank-ment, and head for St Isaac's Square, where the statue of Nicholas I stands. Next, climb the many steps to the top of the massive **St Isaac's Cathedral** (see pp22–3) for a breathtaking view of the city. Later, walk back across St Isaac's Square to **Idiot** (see p70) for a relaxing meal.

Left **Oliva** Centre **Hermitage** Right **A painting adorning the interior of Tandoori Nights**

Restaurants

Da Albertone
A range of delicious pizzas make this pizzeria a great place to come to after visiting the nearby Hermitage. ⊗ *Map M1 • Millionnaya ulitsa 23 • 315 8673 • $$*

Oliva
With Greek interiors, traditional music and authentic Greek menu, Oliva re-creates the feel of Greece. ⊗ *Map L4 • Bolshaya Morskaya ulitsa 31 • 314 6563 • $$$*

Tandoori Nights
This is one of the few places in the city that serves good Indian cuisine. Watch Russians get to grips with the spicy food! ⊗ *Map K4 • Voznesenskiy prospekt 4 • 312 8772 • $$$*

Davidov
One of the city's top restaurants, Davidov has a varied menu and fine location that make it the perfect place for celebrations. ⊗ *Map K4 • Hotel Astoria, Bolshaya Morskaya ulitsa 39 • 494 5757 • $$$$$*

Christopher Columbus
Visit this maritime-themed restaurant for splendid meat and fish dishes, as well as good business lunches. ⊗ *Map L4 • Bolshaya Morskaya ulitsa 27 • 312 9761 • $$*

Gastronom
The eclectic menu here is a mix of Italian, Japanese and Russian cuisine. Enjoy a beer on the pavement tables. ⊗ *Map N2 • Marsovo pole 7 • 318 3849 • $$*

Canvas
The highly recommended Canvas boasts an award-winning chef and a creative menu featuring dozens of mouth-watering dishes. ⊗ *Map K4 • Renaissance Hotel, Pochtamskaya ulitsa 4 • 380 4000 • $$$*

Hermitage
Located right under the arch of the General Staff Building *(see p11)*, this restaurant is a great place for people-watching. The food is average, though attractively served. ⊗ *Map L3 • Palace Square • 314 4772 • $$$*

Idiot
This vegetarian eatery is a St Petersburg favourite, renowned for its excellent business lunches. All guests are given a free shot of vodka. ⊗ *Map K5 • Nab. reki Moyki 82 • 315 1675 • $$$*

Bellevue
Located in the Kempinski Hotel, Bellevue offers fine European-style food and a fantastic view of the city from its wall-to-wall glass windows. ⊗ *Map M2 • Kempinski Hotel, Nab. reki Moyki 22 • 335 9111 • $$$$$*

Some clubs have "face control". This means that a dress code is in place and drunks, or "unsavoury types", will be denied entry.

Price Categories

For a three-course	**US$** under $30
meal for one with half	**US$$** $30–$60
a bottle of wine (or	**US$$$** $60–$90
equivalent meal), taxes	**US$$$$** $90–$120
and extra charges.	**US$$$$$** over $120

Left **Shogun** Right **Buddha Bar's logo**

1 Buddha Bar
A small club-café with house music and good food. It occasionally has theme nights such as *A Journey Through World Cuisine*. ◈ *Map K4 • Bolshaya Morskaya ulitsa 46 • 314 7007 • Adm*

2 Korsar
Korsar, a centrally located club, hosts up-and-coming rock groups, as well as the occasional star. ◈ *Map L3 • Bolshaya Morskaya ulitsa 16 • 318 4184 • Adm for concerts*

3 Museum of the History of Religion
Explore the history of world religions at this fascinating museum. There is an exhibition on Russian Orthodoxy, as well as displays on the Freemasons and other such esoteric movements. ◈ *Map J4 • Pochtamskaya ulitsa 14 • 571 0495 • Open 11am–6pm Thu–Tue • Adm*

4 Novus
A new (some would say gaudy) dance club, Novus plays disco and house. ◈ *Map L3 • Bolshaya Morskaya ulitsa 8 • Adm*

5 Port
Popular with the city's punk and heavy-metal fans, Port often hosts concerts by ageing stars and local groups. ◈ *Map K4 • Antonenko pereulok 2 • 314 2609 • Adm*

6 Shogun
This elegant sushi bar, with its delicious food and good service, was one of the first restaurants to serve Japanese food in St Petersburg when it opened in 1998. ◈ *Map L4 • Gorokhovaya ulitsa 11 • 314 7417 • $$*

7 Astoria Casino
This casino offers a range of games, including fruit machines. There is also a nightclub on the premises. ◈ *Map K4 • Malaya Morskaya ulitsa 22 • 494 5020 • Adm*

8 Shatush
A touch on the expensive side, the elegant Shatush serves "eastern food", including a fine selection of Japanese and Arabic dishes. ◈ *Map L4 • Nab. reki Moyki 64 • 448 6075 • $$$$*

9 Gravitsapa
An atmospheric bar-cum-jazz venue that serves a large range of beer and whisky, and offers a European-style menu. ◈ *Map J4 • Pochtamskaya ulitsa 8 • 312 0343*

10 Astra
While Astra's European and Russian food is strictly okay, its location on a boat moored on the Neva is hard to top. ◈ *Map J3 • Admiralteyskaya nab. 2 • 320 0877 • $$*

Left **Lion Bridge** Right **New Holland**

Sennaya Ploshchad

ONE OF ST PETERSBURG'S OLDEST *residential areas, Sennaya ploshchad was a hotbed of poverty, crime and filth in the 19th century. Dostoevsky (see p34) found the subject matter for his novels in these very streets. An area of sharp contrasts, this part of the city is home to crumbling, century-old houses as well as some of the city's most palatial residences. The tranquil area has much to offer, including the world-famous Mariinskiy Theatre and the stunning St Nicholas' Cathedral. The streets here twist artfully around the Griboedov Canal, the Moyka and the Fontanka.*

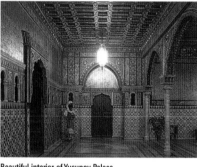

Beautiful interior of Yusupov Palace

🔟 Sights

1. Mariinskiy Theatre
2. The Lion Bridge
3. Yusupov Palace
4. St Nicholas' Cathedral
5. Rimsky-Korsakov Conservatory
6. The English Quay
7. Railway Museum
8. Sennaya Ploshchad
9. New Holland
10. Choral Synagogue

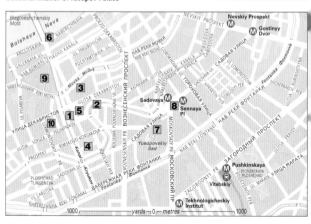

The culturally rich Mariinskiy Theatre

Mariinskiy Theatre
The dazzling Mariinskiy Theatre, also known as the Kirov, has witnessed performances by a number of Russia's most illustrious ballet dancers over the years, including legends such as Nureyev and Nijinsky. Located in Theatre Square, a visit here is a must for any visitor to the city – it is a chance to experience a Russian occasion that remains essentially unchanged since the country's pre-revolutionary days *(see pp16–17)*.

The Lion Bridge
The Lion Bridge, with its elegant, cast-iron lions that hold up the bridge's supports, is a favourite place for couples of all ages to meet before heading off to walk along the atmospheric Griboedov Canal. Dating from the early 19th century, this bridge is a jewel in the heart of Sennaya ploshchad, and one of the city's most recognised landmarks. ✆ *Map J5 • Lvinny most*

Yusupov Palace
Purchased by the wealthy, aristocratic Yusupov family in 1830 to house their personal art collection, the yellow colonnaded Yusupov Palace was designed by Vallin de la Mothe in the 1860s. Its interior is notable for the exotic Moorish Room, with its Islamic-influenced mosaics, arches and fountains. The palace takes its place in history due to the murder of Rasputin *(see p74)*, which took place here in the winter of 1916. The cellar houses an interesting exhibition dedicated to the infamous Rasputin. ✆ *Map J5 • Nab. reki Moyki 94 • 314 9883 • Open 11am–5pm • Adm*

St Nicholas' Cathedral
Overlooking Kryukov Canal, St Nicholas' Cathedral, with its striking sky-blue and white Baroque façade, appears somewhat out of place in the seedy and crumbling streets of Sennaya ploshchad. Completed in 1762, the cathedral was originally intended for sailors and employees of the nearby Admiralty *(see p67)*, and was known for years by residents as the "Sailors' Church". It contains a collection of rare 18th-century icons. ✆ *Map J6 • Nikolskaya ploshchad • 714 0862 • Open 6am–7:30pm*

Baroque façade of St Nicholas' Cathedral

5 Rimsky-Korsakov Conservatory

This is Russia's oldest music school, founded in 1862 by Anton Rubinstein. Notable graduates of the school, before the 1917 Revolution irrevocably changed life in the city, were Tchaikovsky and Prokofiev. During the Soviet period, Dmitriy Shostakovich was its

Railway Museum's exhibits

most famous pupil. Outside the conservatory is a statue of Mikhail Glinka, whose opera, *A Life for the Tsar,* was the first to be performed in Russia in 1836. ⊗ *Map J5 • Teatralnaya ploshchad 3 • 312 2519 • Performances at 7pm • Adm*

6 The English Quay

This collection of buildings gets its name from the English merchants who settled here in the 1730s. They turned the area into a little slice of England and influenced, among other things, the development of football in the city. The mansion at No. 10 featured in Tolstoy's novel *War and Peace,* and No. 28 was once the headquarters of the Socialist Revolutionary Party. ⊗ *Map J3 • Angliyskaya nab.*

The lively Sennaya ploshchad

7 Railway Museum

The museum boasts items that will interest history buffs of all ages, including a fascinating and detailed look at luxury travel in the tsarist era. The museum was established in 1913, and has more than 50,000 exhibits on display, dating from pre-revolutionary Russian carriages to present day engines. ⊗ *Map L6 • Sadovaya ulitsa 50 • 315 1476 • Open 11am–5pm Sun–Thu • Adm*

8 Sennaya Ploshchad

One of the city's oldest squares, Sennaya ploshchad has long had a reputation for poverty and crime. In the 18th century, it was home to the city's cheapest and most picturesque street markets. Soviet authorities

Rasputin

Rasputin was a Russian peasant mystic who, after "miraculously" curing Nicholas II's son of haemophilia, came to exercise considerable, and not entirely benign, influence over the Russian court. On 17 December 1916, a group of nobles, fearful of the control he was exercising, attempted to murder him at Yusupov Palace. Poisoned, shot and clubbed, he eventually succumbed to death, his frozen body recovered from the Neva three days later.

attempted to clean the area up, closing down the market and renaming the square "Ploshchad Mira" ("Peace Square"). Today, while not as dangerous, the square retains elements of its seedy past. ◈ Map L5

9 New Holland

This triangular island gets its name from the Dutch craftsmen who assisted Peter the Great in building the country's first navy. Constructed in 1719 to store timber for the building of ships, the island is today inaccessible and overgrown with weeds. However, there are plans for a grand reopening of the island to the public in 2010, complete with a hotel, a shopping mall, theatres and possibly even a business centre. ◈ Map B5 • Nab. reki Moyki

10 Choral Synagogue

Opened in 1893, this synagogue was the result of the Jewish community's rebirth after years of repression during the reign of Nicholas I. Designed by Ivan Shaposhnikov in Moorish style, it is one of the largest in Europe – its cupola is almost 47 m (154 ft) high. ◈ Map B5
• Lermontovskiy prospekt 2 • 713 8186
• Open 9:30am–6pm

Choral Synagogue

A stroll before a show

Afternoon

🕐 In order to attend an evening performance at the legendary **Mariinskiy Theatre** (see p73), begin your walk at 4pm. Starting at the bustling **Sennaya ploshchad**, head across the road from the exit to Sadovaya Metro station, and walk in the direction of the nab. Kanala Griboedova, turning right after the *Avokado* café (see p78). Turn right again and follow the canal away from the metro towards the 19th-century **Lion Bridge** (see p73), being sure to pay close attention to the magnificently sculpted lions. Take a right at the bridge into the narrow Prachechnyy pereulok, and follow the street to its very end, turning left at the Moyka. Ahead of you is the yellow façade of **Yusupov Palace** (see p73). Audio guides to the palace's interior are available in English and many other languages. Don't forget to check out the exhibition in the basement devoted to the infamous Rasputin.

Evening

After coming out of the Yusupov Palace, follow the Moyka down to Potseluev most (Bridge of Kisses) and take the first left. Ahead of you is **St Nicholas' Cathedral** (see p73). After paying it a visit, retrace your steps back along ulitsa Glinki, named after the 19th-century Russian composer, Mikhail Glinka. It should now be time to take your seats at the Mariinskiy Theatre. After the performance has ended, relax over a filling meal at **Za Tsenoi** (Backstage) (see p76).

Peking's oriental interiors

Restaurants

1 Teatro
This spacious and elegant newcomer serves a wide selection of seafood and Russian dishes and is excellent value. ◎ Map J5 • Glinki ulitsa 2 • 311 1102 • $$

2 Parizh
Parizh (Paris) is a tastefully decorated French restaurant with a good wine list. Serves frog legs with a choice of unusual sauces. ◎ Map J4 • Bolshaya Morskaya 63 • 311 9545 • $$

3 Peking
The menu at this authentic Chinese restaurant is imaginative and prices are reasonable. The most exotic item served here is snake. ◎ Map B5 • Dekabristov ulitsa 27 • 314 1173 • $$

4 Za Tsenoi (Backstage)
Za Tsenoi, which means backstage, is an ideal place for a meal after a performance at the nearby Mariinskiy Theatre. ◎ Map J6 • Next to the Mariinskiy Theatre • 327 0684 • $$$

5 Olimpos
This friendly place is popular for its feta cheese dishes and home-made pies. ◎ Map K5 • Ulitsa Dekabristov 22 • 571 4076 • $$

6 Noble Nest
Kid yourself that you are dining in the tsarist era by trying the authentic imperial dishes on the menu here. ◎ Map J5 • Ulitsa Dekabristov 21 • 312 0911 • $$$$$

7 Rice 2
A cosy Japanese-style café/restaurant, Rice 2 is great value for money. It serves everything you would expect in the way of sushi, along with a large selection of vegetarian and Italian food. Service is fast. ◎ Map M5 • Yefimova ulitsa 3 • 925 1000 • $$

8 Caravan
Sample food from the former Soviet republics of Georgia, Azerbaijan and Uzbekistan. Try the Georgian khachapuri (cheese pastries) or Uzbek plov (fried rice with meat). ◎ Map C6 • Voznesenskiy prospekt 46 • 310 5678 • $$

9 Tsao Van
This Chinese restaurant is ideal for a quick snack and enjoys a fine location on the bank of the Griboedov Canal. ◎ Map K5 • Grazhdanskaya ulitsa 28 • 571 6921 • $

10 Levant
Known for its bizarre snake vodka (snake pickled in vodka), this Chinese eatery serves great business lunches at reasonable prices. ◎ Map K5 • Kazanskaya ulitsa 41 • 314 9629 • $$

Left **Bardak** Centre **Havana Club** Right **Tea Culture Club's serene setting**

⁑10 Clubs

1 Bardak
Famous for its fun-loving crowd, Bardak plays an eclectic mix of music. ⓢ Map L5 • Grivtsova pereulok 11 • Open 8pm–6am • Adm

2 Pyatnitsa (Friday)
Popular with a young crowd. The DJs play mainly drum and bass and hard house. Concerts by local punk groups are regular. ⓢ Map L6 • Moskovskiy prospekt 10/12 • 310 2317 • Open 11pm–6am • Adm

3 Tsinik
A wide range of snacks and occasional live concerts ensure that Tsinik, which features an eclectic mix of music, is packed out at weekends. ⓢ Map K4 • Antonenko pereulok 4 • 312 8779 • Open noon–3am Sun–Fri, noon–6am Sat • Adm for concerts

4 Caramel
Described by its owners as a "sweet R&B club", hence the name, Caramel is a popular hang-out with the young crowd. ⓢ Map L5 • Ulitsa Yefimova 3 • Adm

5 Manhattan
This is a live music club with a great atmosphere and a cheap bar. ⓢ Map N5 • Nab. reki Fontanki 90 • 713 1945 • Open noon–6am • Adm

6 Taxi
Popular with students, Taxi regularly puts on concerts and serves snacks that include dried squid. ⓢ Map C6 • Bronnitskaya ulitsa 4 • 316 7696 • Open noon–1am • Adm

7 Havana Club
This is the centre of the city's Latin Disco/House scene – the place to come if you feel like dancing all night long. ⓢ Map C6 • Moskovskiy prospekt 21 • 259 1155 • Open 5pm–6am • Adm

8 Apollo
A popular house/R&B club that puts on theme nights, including Erotic Night parties at weekends. ⓢ Map C6 • Izmailovskiy 12 • 575 0407 • Open 10pm–6am • Adm

9 Jazz Philharmonic Hall
This sophisticated venue styles itself as the city's answer to the legendary "Birdland" in America. It hosts concerts by established members of St Petersburg's thriving jazz scene. ⓢ Map P5 • Zagorodniy prospekt 27 • 764 8565 • Concerts begin at 7pm

10 Tea Culture Club
Located on the bank of the Fontanka river, this unusual club holds tea ceremonies and sells high-quality Chinese tea. Call ahead for bookings. ⓢ Map M5 • Nab. reki Fontanki 91 • 310 8463 • Open 10am–10pm • Adm for tea ceremonies

Left **The English-style bar, Dickens** Centre **Nebo** Right **Tequila Boom**

🔟 Bars

Dickens
1 This English-style bar has an impressive beer and whisky selection and great food, including breakfast. It also has a restaurant on the first floor. ◈ *Map C5 • Nab. reki Fontanki 108 • 310 6338*

Shamrock
2 The Irish Shamrock, near the Mariinskiy Theatre *(see pp16–17)*, is a St Petersburg institution. It has live music (except on Tue and Fri) – you may even spot a ballerina or two. ◈ *Map B5 • Ulitsa Dekabristov 27 • 570 4625*

Tequila Boom
3 This Mexican bar-restaurant holds theme nights usually involving customers downing large quantities of tequila. ◈ *Map B5 • Voznesenskiy prospekt 57 • 310 1534*

Bier Halle Die Spieler
4 Not exactly a place for a romantic date, this German-style bar is a great choice for beer and snacks with friends. ◈ *Map C5 • Stolyarnny pereulok 13 • 570 4630*

Nebo
5 *Nebo* means "sky" in Russian, and the glass walls of this café-bar allow for maximum exposure. The fine menu includes delicious soups. ◈ *Map C5 • Sennaya ploshchad 2 • 449 2488*

Apollo Sushi Bar
6 Sharing the same building as the Apollo nightclub *(see p77)*, the Apollo Sushi Bar is a cheap place to fill up on sushi before heading off to dance the night away at the club. ◈ *Map C6 • Izmaylovskiy prospekt 12 • 340 0407*

Wasabi-Ko
7 Another popular sushi bar, the elegant Wasabi-Ko also holds tea ceremonies and is well worth a visit. ◈ *Map C5 • Efimova ulitsa 3 • 740 5690*

La Vida Loca
8 Purists may be put off by La Vida Loca's "Russified" menu, but the tequila, tacos and tortillas are hard to resist. ◈ *Map C5 • 39 Gorokhovaya ulitsa • 318 6050*

Pered Boem
9 This 24-hour bar-café-restaurant serves everything from sushi to former Soviet republic of Georgia cuisine. ◈ *Map B6 • 7ya Krasnoarmeyskaya ulitsa 16/3 • 259 9381*

Avocado
10 A sushi bar right across from Sennaya ploshchad metro station, Avocado is great for a quick drink or a snack. ◈ *Map C5 • Sennaya ploshchad 9 • 570 2915*

Russians are among the world's heaviest smokers. Smoking is allowed in most restaurants; non-smokers have a separate area.

Left **Imbir** Centre **Kroshka-Kartoshka's sign** Right **Ro's delicious fare**

🔟 Best of the Rest

1 Umka
Named after the hero of a popular Soviet cartoon, Umka serves draught Russian beer and homemade European food. ◎ *Map C5 • Moskovskiy prospekt 7 • 310 2627*

2 People-watching at Sennaya ploshchad
Day or night, Sennaya ploshchad is a hive of activity. Grab a beer and a pie from a street stall and indulge in some people-watching. ◎ *Map C5*

3 Staroe Kafe
This pleasant café, with its tasty sandwiches, is an ideal place to take a quick break whilst strolling around the Sennaya ploshchad area. ◎ *Map C5 • Nab. reki Fontanki 108 • 316 5111*

4 Gallery of Japanese Art
A fascinating gallery that displays everything from classical art to modern Manga comics. Visits should be booked in advance. ◎ *Map C5 • Nab. reki Fontanki 77 • 901 8118 • Adm*

5 Mu-Mu
Named after a popular Russian children's story, the self-service Mu-Mu serves cheap yet healthy Russian fast food. It gets crowded on weekends. ◎ *Map B6 • Sadovaya ulitsa 94 • 714 5084 • $*

6 Imbir
Imbir (ginger) is a restaurant offering a wide range of cuisines, from European to Eastern. Cosy and laidback, the waiters will not rush you to place your order. ◎ *Map D5 • Zagorodnyy prospekt 15 • 713 3215 • $*

7 Ro
Ro's highlight is its coffee and chocolate cakes. Smoking is prohibited here. ◎ *Moskovskiy prospekt 39 • 575 0002 • $$*

8 Mexx
This popular boutique sells everything from women's clothes to handbags. Although Mex, with a single "x", means fur, there are no fur items on sale here. ◎ *Map C5 • Efimova ulitsa 3 • 449 3902*

9 Kroshka-Kartoshka
This outlet is part of a city-wide chain of food stands that offers baked potatoes with a range of fillings. Popular with vegetarians. ◎ *Map C5 • Efimova ulitsa 3*

10 DVD CD Kiosks
Sennaya ploshchad's tiny kiosks offer DVDs and CDs at knockdown prices. Ensure that the DVDs have English audio tracks before making a purchase. ◎ *Map C5 • Sennaya ploshchad*

For a key to restaurant price categories, see p76

Left **One of the city's sphinxes** Right **The Naval Museum from across the Neva**

Vasilevskiy Island

P ETER THE GREAT ORIGINALLY INTENDED VASILEVSKIY ISLAND, *the largest island in St Petersburg*, to be the administrative centre of his "Window to Europe", but constant flooding and the hazards of crossing the Neva caused him to change his mind. However, the island was not forgotten. Its lower-eastern area, known locally as the Strelka, or Spit, is home to a cluster of fascinating sights, including a pair of eye-catching 15th-century BC sphinxes, the city's first museum and the grand, russet-coloured Rostral Columns. This splendid, detached area of St Petersburg, with its wide, tree-lined avenues, has an exceedingly calm atmosphere.

Sights

1. Rostral Columns
2. Kunstkammer
3. Blagoveshchenskiy Bridge
4. Zoological Museum
5. Naval Museum
6. Academy of Arts
7. Menshikov Palace
8. St Andrew's Cathedral
9. Twelve Colleges
10. Sphinxes

One of the Rostral Columns

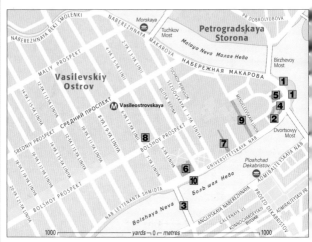

Previous pages **Peterhof**

Kunstkammer

1 Rostral Columns

Flanking the former Stock Exchange (now the Naval Museum), the imposing Rostral Columns (1810) were designed as lighthouses by Thomas de Thomon. The enormous figures sitting at the bases of the two columns represent four of the country's biggest rivers – the Neva, Volga, Dnieper and Volkhov. The columns are decorated in Roman style with ships' prows jutting out from each side. Their gas torches are still lit up on special occasions. ◎ *Map C3 • Birzhevaya ploshchad*

2 Kunstkammer

While the Kunstkammer is notorious for Peter the Great's bizarre collection of deformed foetuses, the museum is also home to an exhaustive Soviet-era exhibition on "The Peoples of the World" – an old-fashioned but informative display of comical waxworks and interesting artifacts. In the main part of the museum, look out for the heart and skeleton of Peter the Great's personal servant, a 2.27-m (7.5-ft) giant, and a display of teeth pulled out by the tsar, who boasted dentistry as his hobby. ◎ *Map K2 • Universitetskaya nab. 3 • 328 1412 • Open 11am–5.45pm Tue–Sun • Adm*

3 Blagoveshchenskiy Bridge

Originally known as the Nicholas Bridge, this bridge (1850) underwent reconstruction work in 1936–8, when it was re-named Lieutenant Shmidt Bridge in honour of the leader of a doomed sailors' uprising in the Black Sea in 1905. It got its current name after extensive re-novation work in 2007. ◎ *Map B4*

4 Zoological Museum

Peter the Great was exceed-ingly fond of stuffed animals and biological mutations. This fine museum contains part of his taxidermical collection, including a horse that the tsar once rode into battle. The museum is one of the largest of its kind in the world, renowned for its stunning collection of mammoths. ◎ *Map B3 • Universitetskaya nab. 1/3 • 328 0112 • Open 11am–6pm Sat–Thu • Adm*

Stuffed polar bears, Zoological Museum

Stalinism

Joseph Stalin (1878–1953) became leader of the Soviet Union in 1922. The dictator led the country through WWII and transformed it into a global super-power. From 1930 onwards, he instigated the "Great Terror" – millions were exiled to labour camps, some never to return. After his death, new Soviet leader Nikita Khrushchev began the process of de-Stalinization.

Naval Museum

This crumbling, yet impress-ive, former stock exchange, with its sculpture of Neptune being drawn in a chariot by sea-horses, was modelled on a famous Greek temple at Paestum in Italy. Transformed into a museum in 1940, it contains an extensive history of the Soviet and Russian navy – the majority of the dis-plays date from the Soviet era. ⊗ Map B3 • Birzhevaya ploshchad 4
• 328 2502 • Open 11am–6pm • Adm
• www.museum.navy.ru

Academy of Arts

The Neo-Classical Academy of Arts (1788) was the birthplace of the Russian Realist art move-ment, whose founders became known as The Wanderers. The group formed in 1863, when 14 discontented students walked out of their exams in protest against the strict conservatism of their lecturers. The academy's students include painter Ilya Repin, and architects Andrey Zakharov and Andrey Voronikhin. Look out for the conference hall's magnificent ceiling painting by Vasiliy Shebuev. ⊗ Map B4
• Universitetskaya nab. 17 • 323 3578
• Open 11am–6pm Wed–Sun • Adm

Menshikov Palace

This Baroque palace (1720) was one of the first stone build-ings in the city. Now a branch of the Hermitage (see pp10–13), it houses an exhibition on 18th-century Russian culture which includes the opulent rooms of Prince Menshikov (1673–1729), who was later exiled to Siberia for treason. While living here, Menshikov entertained regularly and once organized a "dwarf wedding" as amusement for Peter the Great. ⊗ Map B3
• Universitetskaya nab. 15 • 323 1112
• Open 10:30am–4:30pm Tue–Sun • Adm

St Andrew's Cathedral

St Andrew's highlight is its 18th-century iconostasis which includes some extremely rare icons. It stands on the site of a smaller, wooden church, which

The southern façade of Prince Menshikov's 18th-century palace

The iconostasis, St Andrew's Cathedral

was destroyed in 1761 after being struck by lightning. During the WWII siege of the city *(see p32)*, the church's dome housed artillery units. ⊗ *Map A3 • 6-ya Liniya 11 • 323 3418 • Open 9am–9pm*

9 Twelve Colleges
The baroque Twelve Colleges, built between 1722–42, was originally intended to house Russia's 12 government bodies. In 1835 the building, by now empty, was turned over to St Petersburg University. Famous students here include Lenin and eight Nobel Prize winners. Just outside stands a bronze statue of Mikhail Lomonosov (1711–65), Russia's premier Enlightenment scientist. ⊗ *Map B3 • Universitetskaya nab. 7 • Closed to public*

10 Sphinxes
This pair of 15th-century BC sphinxes was discovered in Thebes in ancient Egypt in the mid-19th century and later brought to St Petersburg. A local landmark, the sphinxes' faces are said to resemble Pharaoh Amenhotep II. ⊗ *Map B4*

A Day Exploring the Strelka

Morning

All the main sights on Vasilevskiy Island are relatively close, so there is no need for public transport or excruciatingly long walks. Start the morning at the 19th-century **Rostral Columns**, admiring the view across the Neva. Perhaps St Petersburg's defining feature, the river lies frozen in winter. Afterwards, cross over the road to Universitetskaya nab. and walk down to the city's oldest museum, the **Kunstkammer** *(see p83)*. Spend some time exploring Peter the Great's mania for biological oddities. When you have sufficiently recovered your nerve, walk the short distance towards the **Academy of Arts**, home of the Russian Realist art movement. Directly across the road from the Academy are the **Sphinxes**, standing guard on the riverside. The sphinxes are a meeting point for the city's youth. Buy a momento from the numerous souvenir sellers here, and then stroll towards **Blagoveshchenskiy Bridge**, which was extensively renovated in 2007.

Noon

Now walk down to the splendid 18th-century **St Andrew's Cathedral** – admire its breathtaking iconostasis. Afterwards, go back to Universitetskaya nab. and drop in at **Russian Kitsch** *(see p86)* for a slightly surreal journey back to the Soviet era, complete with Soviet pop and menus bound in the works of Lenin.

Left **Maskarad** Centre **A delicious cake served at Lido** Right **1703's interesting decor**

Around Town – Vasilevskiy Island

TOP 10 Restaurants

1 Russian Kitsch
This ironic *perestroika*-themed restaurant serves a delicious mix of fusion and sushi. Stunning views across the Neva from the sushi bar are another draw. ✪ *Map A4 • Universitetskaya nab. 25 • 325 1122 • $$$$*

2 Old Customs House
Drop in here after a visit to the Kunstkammer *(see p83)*, if Peter the Great's hobby hasn't spoilt your appetite. The menu is strongly based around French cuisine. ✪ *Map B4 • Tamozhenny pereulok 1 • 327 8980 • $$$$*

3 Fu Tyan
Excellently located near the Blagoveshchenskiy Bridge *(see pp83)*, this Chinese restaurant offers tasty business lunches. ✪ *Map B3 • 1-ya liniya 6 • 328 2687 • $$*

4 Maskarad
Close to Vasileostrovskaya metro station, friendly Maskarad (Masquerade) serves European and Russian food. ✪ *Map A3 • 4-ya liniya 13 • 718 3719 • $*

5 Chardash
One of the few Hungarian restaurants in Russia, this stylish bistro overlooks the Neva. Try the *Tokaj* (Hungarian wine). ✪ *Map A3 • Makarova nab. 22 • 323 8588 • $$*

6 Angel
Dine here for delicious Mediterranean food in a bright and relaxed setting. The ice-creams here are particularly good. There is also a bar on the 2nd floor. ✪ *Map A3 • 1-ya liniya 36 • 327 7444 • $$$*

7 1703
Named after the founding year of St Petersburg, this restaurant serves a mixture of European and Russian food, plus on-tap local beer. ✪ *Map A3 • 9-ya liniya 54 • 320 6964 • $$*

8 Bogemus
This Czech bar-restaurant-disco right next to the Neva has light and dark beer on tap, including Krusovice, the Czech Republic's finest beer. ✪ *Map B3 • Makarova nab. 10 • 323 9286 • $$*

9 Osio
It might be a little out of the way, but Osio serves superb Asian food, including sushi. ✪ *Map A3 • Malyy prospekt 49 • 328 3994 • $$*

10 Lido
A stylish establishment next to the metro, Lido boasts an impressive selection of cakes and other desserts. ✪ *Map A3 • 6-ya liniya 29 • 328 2639*

Only restaurants in top hotels are sure to accept credit cards, so carry plenty of cash when going out for an evening meal.

Price Categories

For a three-course	
meal for one with half	**US$** under $30
a bottle of wine (or	**US$$** $30–$60
equivalent meal), taxes	**US$$$** $60–$90
and extra charges.	**US$$$$** $90–$120
	US$$$$$ over $120

Left **Black and White interiors** Right **A wedding celebration by the Rostral Columns**

10 Best of the Rest

1 Black and White
Right next to the metro, Black and White serves good, if slightly overpriced coffee. Computers with fast internet connections can be used for a fee. ✎ Map A3 • 6-ya liniya 25 • 323 3881

2 Celebrating at the Rostral Columns
During the summer, the city becomes one huge street café as locals and tourists gather at spots like this to socialize. Weddings also take place here. ✎ Map C3 • Birzhevaya ploshchad

3 Russian Billiard Club "Vint"
Vint is a great place to drink beer and get to grips with the local version of the game. ✎ Map A3 • 15-ya liniya 32 • 323 3057 • Adm

4 Red Cube
Red Cube, a fashionable shop selling items such as clocks, mugs and ornaments is a good place to buy a gift. ✎ Map A3 • Sredniy prospekt 26/28 • 323 1993

5 Ostrov
This dance club resembles a sunny tropical island. Pop bands Modern Talking and A-Ha have dropped in here on visits to the city. ✎ Map A4 • Nab. Leytenanta Shmidta 37 • 946 0058 • Adm

6 Fitness House Plaza
Opened in 2000, Plaza is one of the city's best equipped fitness centres. It has a spa,

sauna facilities and excellent training halls. ✎ Map B3 • Nab. Admirala Makarova 2 • 323 9090 • Adm • www.fitnesshouse.spb.ru

7 Star Café
This trendy 24-hour café mixes its own original cocktails. Some of the city's most popular DJs play here on weekends. ✎ Map A3 • Sredniy prospekt 46 • 325 2655

8 Jambala
Jambala offers Russian reggae and sometimes even hosts concerts by authentic Jamaican reggae musicians. ✎ Map A4 • Bolshoy prospekt 80 • 332 1077 • Adm

9 Greenwich
Designed to look like a London club, Greenwich serves a wide range of imported beers and draws a hip crowd. ✎ Map B3 • Nab. Admirala Makarova 2 (at Fitness House Plaza entrance) • 982 1834

10 Biergarten
A cosy German-style pub – the ideal place for relaxing over a mug of beer and relishing a hearty meal. ✎ Map A3 • 6-ya liniya 15 • 329 0895 • $$$

Left **Kshesinskaya Mansion** Right **A summer day at Aleksandrovskiy Park**

Petrogradskaya

*A*LTHOUGH THE FOUNDING OF THE CITY *dates from the construction of the Peter and Paul Fortress, Petrogradskaya was sparsely populated until the building of Trinity Bridge in 1903, when the area became accessible from the centre of the city. It quickly became one of the city's most popular spots. During the ensuing building boom, many Style-Moderne buildings were commissioned, a trend which helped to shape the area's present-day character and atmosphere. While the Peter and Paul Fortress is the main tourist highlight, Petrogradskaya, with its iconic Cruiser* Aurora *and exotic*

Sobornaya Mosque, is rich in cultural and architectural delights. From the desolate swampland where Peter the Great chose to found his city to today's elegant, residential area, Petrogradskaya has come a long way.

Lion guarding Peter's Cabin

Sights

1. Peter and Paul Fortress
2. Trinity Square
3. Artillery Museum
4. Kirov Museum
5. Kshesinskaya Mansion
6. Cruiser Aurora
7. Aleksandrovskiy Park
8. Sobornaya Mosque
9. Manchurian Lions
10. Cabin of Peter the Great

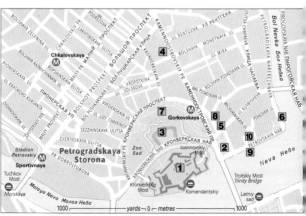

Peter and Paul Fortress

This fortress is where Peter the Great once strolled, dreaming of the city to come, where Dostoevsky *(see p34)* was imprisoned for his political beliefs and where Nicholas II *(see p33)* was laid to rest decades after his execution. The Baroque Cathedral of SS Peter and Paul here forms a magnificent setting for the tombs of the Romanov monarchs *(see pp20–21)*.

Trinity Square

Trinity Square, known as Revolution Square during the Soviet era *(see p53)*, owes its name to the Church of the Trinity which once stood here. Built in 1710 and destroyed in the 1930s during the USSR's anti-religion campaign, the church served the area's merchants. Stretching from the square, across the widest point of the Neva river, is the elegant Trinity Bridge *(see p54)*, whose construction transformed the area's fate by connecting it to the rest of the city. Map D2 • Troitskaya ploshchad

The Peter and Paul Fortress

Artillery Museum

Along with the Kunstkammer *(see p83)*, this is one of St Petersburg's oldest museums,

Trinity Bridge crossing the Neva

An exhibit outside the Artillery Museum

with plans for its foundation dating from the construction of the city in 1703. The museum contains hundreds of weapons, many of them dating back to medieval times; a majority of the exhibitions are connected in some way with Russia's victorious 1812 war against Napoleon. Built between 1849–60, the museum is housed in a horseshoe-shaped, red-brick building designed by the Russian architect, Pyotr Tamanskiy. Map C2 • Aleksandrovskiy Park 7 • 232 0296 • Open 11am–5pm Wed–Sun; closed Mon, Tue and last Thu • Adm

Kirov Museum

The downfall of the Soviet politician Sergey Kirov was his popularity, which led Stalin to have him murdered in 1934. This event sparked off the Great Terror of the 1930s, during which executions became a fact of life *(see p33)*. Kirov's flat, which houses the museum, has been preserved just as it was during his lifetime, and contains documents and photographs chronicling his political career. Map C1 • Kamennoostrovskiy prospekt 26–28 • 346 0289 • Open 11am–6pm Thu–Tue • Adm • www.spbmuseum.ru

Kshesinskaya Mansion

This stylish mansion was once the home of Matilda Kshesinskaya, a ballerina at the Mariinskiy Theatre *(see pp16–17)* during the late 19th century and lover of the future Nicholas II. The mansion was designed for her by the then court architect, A Von Gogen. It became the headquarters of the Bolsheviks during the early days of the 1917 Revolution, and now houses the Museum of Russian Political History *(see p53)*. ◈ *Map D2 • Ulitsa Kuybysheva 4 • 233 7052 • Open 10am–6pm Fri–Wed • Adm*

Cruiser Aurora

On 25 October 1917 at 9:40pm, the cruiser *Aurora* gave the signal for the storming of the Winter Palace by firing a blank round from the bow gun. At the beginning of the siege of the city *(see p32)*, the ship was sunk to protect it from the Nazis. Raised

Cruiser *Aurora*

The huge Sobornaya Mosque

from the depths in 1944, the *Aurora* would no longer see active service. It has been a museum since 1956. ◈ *Map D2 • Petrogradskaya nab. 4 • 230 8440 • Open 10:30am–4pm; closed Mon and Fri • Adm*

Aleksandrovskiy Park

The one-time cultural centre of the Petrogradskaya area, this park was home to varying forms of entertainment during the 20th century, including performances in the Opera House (1911) and clown and animal acts in the People's House, which was founded by Nicholas II in 1900. The park still draws crowds today. It is home to the zoo, the planetarium and the Music Hall, formerly the Opera House, which hosts pop concerts. ◈ *Map C2 • Aleksandrovskiy Park*

Sobornaya Mosque

One of Europe's largest mosques, Sobornaya Mosque can hold up to 5,000 people. Constructed in 1913 by Nikolai Vasiliev and Stepan Krichinskiy with money collected by Russian Muslims, the mosque has a sky-blue cupola and minarets, and a grey granite exterior. Used as a warehouse during much of the Soviet period, the mosque is

ack in service today. Access to
he mosque is limited for non-
Muslims, although it is possible
o gain entry when prayers are
not taking place. ◈ *Map C2*
• *Kamennoostrovskiy prospekt 7 • 233
3819 • Open 10am–5pm*

9 **Manchurian Lions**
This pair of unusual frog-
lions, which stand opposite the
cabin of Peter the Great on the
water's edge, were brought from
the Manchurian town of Gurin
during the Russo-Japanese War
of 1904–05. A local landmark,
they were presented to the city
by General Grodevok in 1907, and
are known in St Petersburg as
the Shih Tzsa (Chinese for lion).
◈ *Map D2 • Petrovskaya nab. 6*

10 **Cabin of Peter the Great**
Built from scratch in just
three days in May 1703, this was
the city's first building. Peter the
Great, never one for luxury, lived
here for six years, overseeing
the construction of his city. The
protective brick walls were
added later by Catherine the
Great. A fascinating museum
containing some of Peter's
personal possessions, including
his compass, clothes and rowing
boat, now occupies the building.
◈ *Map D2 • Petrovskaya nab. 6 • 232
4576 • Open 10am–6pm Wed–Sun,10am–
4pm Mon • Adm*

Inside the Cabin of Peter the Great

A Walk Through History

Morning

🕐 Start at Gorkovskaya
metro station and,
crossing the road via the
underpass, walk down
Kamennoostrovskiy
prospekt to **Sobornaya
Mosque**, using its sky-
blue minarets and cupola
to guide you – you may
be lucky enough to be
allowed a look inside. After
that, walk down to **Trinity
Square** *(see p89)* and
admire the elegant **Trinity
Bridge** *(see p54)*. Without
crossing the bridge, turn
left and take a stroll along
Petrovskaya nab., admiring
the views of the Neva. A
short distance from Trinity
Bridge is the **Cabin of
Peter the Great**. Visit the
museum inside and as
you leave, don't miss the
Manchurian Lions on the
bank just opposite. Stop
for lunch at the **Volna**
(Wave) *(see p92)*.

Afternoon

After eating, stroll back
to Kamennoostrovskiy
prospekt and on to the
Peter and Paul Fortress
(see pp20–21). A visit
here will take up the rest
of the afternoon. Be sure
to see the magnificent
**Cathedral of SS Peter
and Paul**, seeking out the
tombs of the Romanov
monarchs. A visit to the
Trubetskoy Bastion, the
home of countless famous
prisoners down the years,
is also not to be missed. If
you have time, stop by to
observe the controversial
1991 **Statue of Peter the
Great** outside Neva Gate,
from which point prisoners
were exiled or sent off for
execution. After all that
history, if the weather is
good, head over to the
beach for sunbathing and
a beer or two.

Left **Austeria** Centre **Volna (Wave)** Right **Edo**

Around Town – Petrogradskaya

🔟 Restaurants

Demyanova Ukha
This fine seafood restaurant, which takes its name from a Russian fairy tale, cooks up good traditional food. ⊗ Map C2 • Kronverskiy prospekt 53 • 232 8090 • $$

Austeria
Drop in for wholesome local dishes in an interior that re-creates Peter the Great's favoured Dutch style. ⊗ Map C2 • Peter and Paul Fortress • 230 0369 • $$$

Porter House
Choose from a vast range of whiskies and imported beers to go along with the great seafood and salads served here. ⊗ Map C2 • Voskova ulitsa 31 • 233 3352 • $$

Volna (Wave)
Volna is a fusion restaurant that features excellent fish dishes. It also has a selection of divine desserts. ⊗ Map D2 • Petrovskaya nab. 4 • 322 5383 • $$$

Cherdak (Attic)
A cosy place for an evening meal, Cherdak serves mainly European dishes and service is fast and friendly. The cocktails here are worth a try. ⊗ Map D1 • Ulitsa Kuybysheva 38/40 • 232 1102 • $$$

Amazonki
European-style dishes are served here with salads that betray hints of an Asian influence. There is also a bamboo bar serving great cocktails. ⊗ Map D1 • Ulitsa Chapaeva 4 • 232 9706 • $$

Na Dvoryanskoi
A good-value restaurant that offers large portions of simple yet tasty Russian dishes, as well as local beer on tap. ⊗ Map D1 • Ulitsa Kuybysheva 21 • 233 0476 • $$

Edo
An enthusiastic, if not entirely authentic, sushi bar. A cheap place for a quick snack if you happen to be passing by, but not a restaurant for Japanese food purists. ⊗ Map D2 • Ulitsa Kuybysheva 7 • 233 9468 • $

Aquarel
The pricey Aquarel boasts a superb fusion menu and spec-tacular views of the Neva, along with a high-tech, lavish interior. ⊗ Map B2 • Birezhevoy Most • 320 8600 • $$$$$

Povari
Povari may look like a fast-food joint, but it is actually a quality Italian restaurant serving good pasta and fine salads, but no pizza. With its comfortable terrace, this eatery comes highly recommended. ⊗ Map B2 • Bolshoi prospekt 38/40 • 233 7042 • $$$

Price Categories

For a three-course meal for one with half a bottle of wine (or equivalent meal), taxes and extra charges.	**US$** under $30
	US$$ $30–$60
	US$$$ $60–$90
	US$$$$ $90–$120
	US $$$$$ over $120

Morkovka

🔟 Best of the Rest

Parking
1 A popular nightclub, Parking attracts an energetic crowd with its dance pop and chill-out halls. ◎ *Map C2 • Alexandrovskiy Park 4V (4B in Russian) • 498 0606 • Adm*

MIXbar
2 A club that features occasional live music, MIXbar was founded by one of Russia's most famous promoters. Its DJs spin mainly house music. ◎ *Map B1 • Bolshoi prospekt 82 • 313 1951 • Adm*

Mirage Cinema
3 With a sushi bar, billiards and an Internet centre, this cinema is a great place to catch up on new releases. ◎ *Map B1 • Bolshoy prospekt 35 • 498 0563 • Adm • www.mirage.ru*

Flying Dutchman
4 The Flying Dutchman, or *Letuchiy Gollandets*, is a club-restaurant that serves good beer. Its menu is an eclectic mix of world cuisines. ◎ *Map B2 • Mytinskaya nab. 6 • 336 3737*

Kamchatka
5 Expect lots of black leather and moody music at this live music club inspired by Viktor Tsoi, leader of the *perestroika*–era group Kino. ◎ *Map B2 • Ulitsa Blokhina 15 • 498 0887 • Adm*

Tunnel
6 The adventurous Tunnel, located in an old bomb shelter, features hip DJs and live music and is one of St Petersburg's most happening clubs. ◎ *Map B2 • Corner of Zverinskaya ulitsa and Lubanskovo pereulok • 233 4015 • Adm*

Petrovskiy
7 Watch Zenit, the city's top-level football club, in action at this stadium. ◎ *Map A2 • Petrovskiy Ostrov • 328 8903 • www.fc-zenit.ru*

The Riverbank
8 The beach just beyond the walls of the Peter and Paul Fortress *(see pp20–21)*, with its views of the Neva, is perfect for a lazy afternoon. ◎ *Map C2 • Petropavlovskaya Krepost*

Morkovka
9 A popular health-food café that serves freshly squeezed juices and low-fat food – a good option for vegetarians. ◎ *Map B1 • Bolshoy prospekt 32 • 233 9635 • $$*

Jean Jacques Rousseau
10 This stylish, authentic French-style café boasts a long wine and spirits list, and dishes up some delicious desserts. A treat for Francophiles. ◎ *Map B1 • Bolshoy prospekt 54 • 232 9981 • $$$*

Left **Cathedral of the Transfiguration** Centre **Gulf of Finland** Right **Locomotive at Finland Station**

Further Afield

THE OUTSKIRTS OF ST PETERSBURG, *while largely lacking the Imperial elegance of the centre, still offer a lot in terms of architecture and historical monuments. The east of the city is dominated by the Smolnyy district, including the Smolnyy Institute, which played a significant role in events immediately following the 1917 Revolution (see p32). To the north lies Finland Station, containing the train that brought Lenin home to Russia from exile in 1917. To the south is the mainly residential area of Moskovskaya ploshchad, the district that Stalin, rejecting Nevskiy prospekt's tsarist trappings, attempted to make into the new city centre. Sitting on the city's far southern outskirts is the splendid Neo-Gothic Chesma Church and the 1970s Victory Monument, a homage to the darkest days of WWII, dedicated to the siege victims.*

Mother Russia, Piskarevskoe Memorial Cemetery

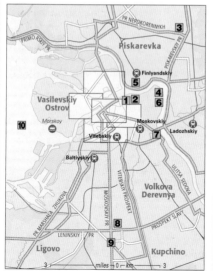

Sights

1. Stieglitz Museum
2. Cathedral of the Transfiguration
3. Piskarevskoe Memorial Cemetery
4. Smolnyy Convent
5. Finland Station
6. Smolnyy Institute
7. Alexander Nevskiy Monastery
8. Chesma Church
9. Victory Monument
10. Gulf of Finland

Around Town – Further Afield

Stieglitz Museum

The Stieglitz Museum (1896) was originally the Central School of Industrial Design and, after WWII, it became a training centre for craftsmen. Today, it contains an exhibition of wood and metalwork, including locks and keys from the Middle Ages. The highlights are the intricately decorated Terem Room and the Grand Exhibition Hall, with its elegant marble staircase and dazzling glass roof. ✆ Map P2 • Solyanoy pereulok 13 • 273 3258 • Open Aug–May 11am–4:30pm Tue–Sat • Adm

Inside the Stieglitz Museum

Cathedral of the Transfiguration

The original church that stood on this site burnt to the ground in 1825, but the icons and iconostases were rescued. Today's Neo-Classical structure, consecrated in August 1829, is famous for its choir. The fence around the cathedral is made of cannons captured during Russia's 18th-century military campaigns against the Turks. ✆ Map E3 • Preobrazhenskaya ploshchad 1 • 272 3662 • Open 8am–8pm daily

Piskarevskoe Memorial Cemetery

During the WWII siege of the city (see p32), thousands of corpses were transported on sledges to cemeteries in the outskirts of town – Piskarevskoe was the largest of these. Containing an exhibition hall and a giant bronze statue of Mother Russia, the cemetery is a stark reminder of the horrors of war. ✆ Map H1 • Prospekt Nepokorennykh 74 • 247 5716 • Memorial exhibition: Open 10am–5pm

Smolnyy Convent

Tsarina Elizabeth founded this convent in 1748 and planned to see out her old age in it. However, she died before its completion. Upon the ascension of Catherine the Great, the convent was turned into Russia's first girls' school. A stunning 19th-century cathedral with a dome and cupolas topped by gold orbs is the structure's crowning glory. ✆ Map G2 • Ploshchad Rastrelli 3/1 • 577 1422 • Open 10am–5pm Tue–Thu

Façade of the Smolnyy Cathedral with adjacent buildings of the Smolnyy Convent

Finland Station

5 Finland Station was a place of pilgrimage for hordes of Party members during Russia's years of Soviet rule. On 3 April 1917, the exiled Lenin and his Bolshevik companions returned from Switzerland to a triumphant reception at Finland Station. Forced again to flee the country for the summer, they returned in the autumn, once more to Finland Station, and spurred the 1917 Revolution *(see p32)*.
✆ *Map E2 • Ploshchad Lenina 6*

Smolnyy Institute

6 This Neo-Classical building houses the Mayor of St Petersburg's office, but during the days following the 1917 Revolution, it was the seat of govern- ment. Lenin ruled from here until the advancing German troops and the outbreak of civil war forced him to move the capital to Moscow. Leon Trotsky (1879–1940), who later fell out with Stalin and was murdered in Mexico by a Soviet agent, also worked here, heading the City Soviet Council. ✆ *Map G3 • Ploshchad Proletarskoy Diktatury • 276 1746 • Open 10am–5pm Mon–Fri • Adm*

St Petersburg vs. Moscow

As is the case in many "second cities" all over the world, St Petersburg's residents often favourably compare their home- town to the capital of the country. Moscow, say the locals, is a "big village", a hectic city where money rules supreme. St Petersburg, on the other hand, is said to be a town of calm, polite intellectuals.

Alexander Nevskiy Monastery

7 This sprawling monastery- complex was founded in 1710 by Peter the Great on the supposed site of the 1240 battle between Russia and Sweden. It contains the early 18th- century Cathedral of the Annunciation, as well as the twin-towered and domed Neo- Classical Holy Trinity Cathedral, home to the remains of Nevskiy, a revered 16th-century saint of

Alexander Nevskiy Monastery

Russia. The monastery is also home to two cemeteries, Lazarus and Tikhvin, the latter containing the graves of Dostoevsky *(see p34)* and the 19th-century composer Pyotr Tchaikovsky. ✆ *Map G5 • Ploshchad Aleksandra Nevskogo • 274 2635 • Open 9:30am–5pm Wed–Sun*

Chesma Church

8 The Neo-Gothic Chesma Church, with its wedding- cake, terracotta- coloured façade, is one of the city's most distinctive churches. Built between 1777–80, it was named in honour of the

Smolnyy Institute

Chesma Church

Russian naval victory over Turkey at Chesma in 1770 and used as a museum dedicated to the battle during the Soviet era. Opposite the church is the Neo-Gothic Chesma Palace, which was built between 1774–7. ⊗ *Map H1*
• *Ulitsa Lensoveta 12* • *Open 10am–7pm*

9 Victory Monument

The Siege of Leningrad *(see p32)* had a colossal effect upon the mentality of the survivors *(blokadniki)* and upon the nature of the city itself. This monument, dedicated to the victims of the *blokada* (blockade), both alive and dead, consists of massive, resolute figures carved from granite – an image that will linger long after you have left the city. ⊗ *Map H1* • *Ploshchad Pobedi*

10 Gulf of Finland

The Gulf of Finland, at the west of the city, is an important shipping lane into which the Neva river drains. Visitors to the city will fall in love with the fantastic views it affords, especially in winter, when a stroll along the coast is akin to an expedition into the frozen wastelands of the North Pole. ⊗ *Map H1*

Three Excursions

Trip 1

At the vast **Piskarevskoe Memorial Cemetery** *(see p95)*, start with a visit to the Siege of Leningrad exhibition hall. Then make your way down the avenue leading to the heroic Mother Russia statue. Those able to read Russian should examine the verses on the wall behind, composed by a survivor of the Siege *(see p32)*. The 186 grassy mounds located on either side of the avenue are mass graves containing the bodies of the Siege victims. A red star indicates that the graves hold soldiers; a hammer and sickle, civilians.

Trip 2

Begin your visit at the **Victory Monument** and spend some time taking in the symbolic 48-m (157-ft) high granite obelisk before wandering among the colossal sculptures depicting the suffering brought to the city by WWII. Then make your way through the dimly lit underpass to the Memorial Hall. Inside the hall, look out for the display that contains a tiny crust of bread – the daily ration during the Seige.

Trip 3

Walk down the Neva embankment towards **Ploshchad Lenina**, where the famous 1926 **Statue of Lenin** stands *(see p52)*. Next, walk across to **Finland Station** to see the train that brought Lenin to Russia to lead the 1917 Revolution. After this, wander over to the nearby **Ploshchad Lenina Metro Station**, where you can take in an intricate Soviet-era Lenin mosaic.

The way to the Memorial Hall at the Victory Monument is lined with 900 dim, orange lamps, one for each day of the Siege.

97

Left **Lagidze** Centre **Rice** Right **Probka**

🔟 Restaurants

1 Lagidze
Opened at the end of the 1970s, when restaurants were rare in the city, Lagidze serves good, tasty Georgian food. 🔊 *Map E3 • Ulitsa Belinskovo 3 • 579 1104 • $$*

2 Sphinx
A relatively new restaurant-café, Sphinx is an excellent place to come to for generous portions at cheap prices. The lasagna dishes are especially good. 🔊 *Map E4 • Nevskiy prospekt 118 • 717 6868 • $*

3 Staraya Derevnaya
Staraya Derevnaya, which means "Old Village", was one of St Petersburg's very first independent restaurants. It serves unpretentious Russian and European dishes. 🔊 *Ulitsa Savushkina 72 • 431 0000 • $$*

4 Rice
Serving mainly Japanese food and alcohol, including plum wine and sake, Rice is open until 5am – perfect during the White Nights *(see p102)*. 🔊 *Map E3 • Vosstaniya ulitsa 55 • 272 7215 • $$*

5 Hunters' Club
Dine on traditional Russian food accompanied by Russian beer on tap. 🔊 *Map G3 • Novgorodskaya ulitsa 27 • 327 8274 • $$$*

6 Kolhida
Great for a meal before or after visiting the nearby Alexander Nevskiy Monastery, Kolhida specializes in Georgian dishes, including *lobio* (spicy red beans) and fine wines. 🔊 *Map G5 • Nevskiy prospekt 176 • 274 2514 • $$$$*

7 Probka
A sophisticated Italian wine bar-restaurant, Probka serves delicious pasta dishes, but no pizza. 🔊 *Map E3 • Ulitsa Belinskovo 5 • 273 4904 • $$$$*

8 Edinburgh
Despite its name, you will not get to eat any traditional Scottish food at Edinburgh, a European restaurant close to the Victory Monument. 🔊 *Map H1 • Moskovskiy prospekt 195 • 371 9078 • $$*

9 Hande Hoch!
This is a typical German-style beer hall-restaurant with wooden tables, frankfurters, and good on-tap beer. 🔊 *Map F4 • Grechiskiy prospekt 2 • 710 3452 • $$$*

10 Ditai
A restaurant boasting chefs from Beijing, Detai offers a range of green teas and Asian food other than sushi. 🔊 *Lesnoy prospekt 4 • 542 6440 • $$$*

Price Categories

For a three-course	**US$** under $30
meal for one with half	**US$$** $30–$60
a bottle of wine (or	**US$$$** $60–$90
equivalent meal), taxes	**US$$$$** $90–$120
and extra charges.	**US$$$$$** over $120

Derzhis

^{TOP}10 Clubs and Bars

1 Red Club
This dance music club often puts on live concerts. DJs here spin house and techno. ◈ *Map E3*
• *Ulitsa Poltavskaya 7 • 717 0000*
• *Concerts start at 7pm • Adm*

2 Metro
Spread over many levels, Metro plays the phenomenon that is Russian domestic pop and hosts karaoke nights. ◈ *Map E6 • Ligovskiy prospekt 174 • 766 0204 • Adm*

3 Che
Che offers cocktails and music round the clock and also puts on live jazz concerts. ◈ *Map F5 • Ulitsa Poltavskaya 3 • 717 7600*

4 IQ
With its on-tap beer and proximity to Ploshchad Vosstaniya metro, IQ is the ideal place to start, or end, the night. ◈ *Map F5 • Nevskiy prospekt 158 • 277 4972 • Adm*

5 Deep Sound
Located in a former bomb shelter, Deep Sound features electronic music DJs, who play drum and bass, techno and trip hop. ◈ *Map E6 • Ulitsa Chernyakhovskovo 31 • 572 1111 • Adm*

6 Griboedov
Another club in a bomb shelter, this arty, underground venue is one of the oldest in the city. It hosts live concerts and has experimental DJs. Worth checking out. ◈ *Map E6*
• *Voronezhskaya 2A • 764 4355 • Adm*

7 Decadence
With a gold ceiling and decorated bar, Decadence attracts a fun-loving crowd. It is considered to have the best sound system in St Petersburg. ◈ *Map E5 • Sherbakov pereulok 17 • 947 7070 • Adm*

8 Derzhis
A slick cocktail bar with over 400 varieties, Derzhis also offers custom-made cocktails on request. ◈ *Map E3 • Ulitsa Mayakovskaya 56 • 272 0970*

9 City Bar
City Bar is extremely popular with St Petersburg's expat crowd for its large, good-value breakfasts and wide selection of imported beers. ◈ *Map E3 • Ulitsa Furshtatskaya 20 • 448 5837*

10 Foggy Dew
This authentic-looking Irish bar serves good, if slightly overpriced, lunches, has very friendly bar staff and offers good service. Locals and expats as well as tourists flock here on weekends. ◈ *Map E3 • Ulitsa Vosstaniya 39 • 273 6263*

STREETSMART

ST PETERSBURG'S TOP 10

Left **The frozen Neva river during winter** Right **Tourists exploring the city**

Planning Your Visit

1 When to Go
The peak time to visit the city is from 11 Jun–2 Jul, during White Nights, when the sun never quite sets. Failing this, the weather during late May–Aug is usually good. If it is snow and ice you are after, then mid-Jan to end-Feb is ideal.

2 National Holidays
The main national holidays include: 1 Jan, New Year's Day; 7 Jan, Russian Orthodox Christmas; 23 Feb, Defenders of the Motherland Day; Mar/Apr, Easter Sunday; 8 Mar, International Women's Day; 1 May, Labour Day; 9 May, Victory Day; 12 Jun, Russia Day; 4 Nov, Day of National Unity; 7 Nov, Day of Reconciliation; 12 Dec, Constitution Day.

3 Length of Stay
A week to nine days is plenty of time to see most of the main sights in the city without having to rush. However, shorter periods, even a weekend during White Nights, are enough to get a proper feel for St Petersburg.

4 Visas & Passports
All foreign visitors must obtain a visa before travelling to Russia, and passports must be valid for a minimum of 6 months after the expiry date. Visa applications can be submitted in person at a Russian consulate, by an agent or by mail. Independent travellers must provide proof of their hotel reservation and those visitors staying at private homes need to produce an official invitation from their host. Detailed information on how to make a visa application depending on your nationality can be found at www.rusemblon.org

5 What to Bring
If you are travelling in winter, then take warm clothes and thick, waterproof boots. Most goods are available in St Petersburg, although if you are on prescribed medication, you should bring enough to last the entire duration of your trip. English language books can be found in the city, although the choice is fairly limited.

6 Local Prices
Clothes are more expensive in Russia than in the US or UK. Basic food items, such as bread, are very cheap and public transport is incredibly good value. There are no bargains to be had on electronic items and foreigners are often charged up to 15 times more than Russians for entrance to top sights.

7 Language
Russian is a very complex language, but it is not difficult to learn a few polite phrases before setting off on your trip. The Russian language uses the Cyrillic alphabet, which is fairly easy to grasp at a basic level. Given that many English words are in use in Russia, a little knowledge of the Cyrillic alphabet can come in very handy.

8 Electricity
The electrical current is 220 V. The plugs are two-pin, but some of the older sockets do not accept standard European plugs. Adaptors are cheaply available in shops that sell electrical items, though it may be a good idea to take a couple with you to save time.

9 Travelling with Children
Children under five travel free on the metro and are entitled to free entry to museums. The city, however, is not exactly brimming over with attractions for children. Old Russian women are very fond of giving parents advice along the lines of "Put a hat on that child!", especially during winter.

10 Disabled Travellers
The city is severely lacking in facilities for the disabled. Only luxury hotels and the very top restaurants can be relied on to have facilities. It would be inadvisable for a disabled person to travel here alone – even with a helper, it would take a lot of effort.

For details on agencies that assist with visa applications, visit www.russianvisa.net

Left **A Pulkovo airplane** Right **New building at Pulkovo 2**

🔟 Getting to St Petersburg

1 Arriving by Air at Pulkovo 2

Pulkovo 2 is the city's international airport, yet it is relatively small and underdeveloped. The queues can be long during weekends. You will find duty-free shops and foreign exchange offices in the departure and arrival halls.

2 Arriving by Air at Pulkovo 1

The Pulkovo 1 is exclusively used for domestic and charter international flights. Flights to and from Moscow have separate arrival and departure lounges. The rates at the foreign exchange booths here, as at Pulkovo 2, are not as good as those in the main city.

3 Russian Airlines

Russian airlines suffer from an image problem. However, Rossiya, Aeroflot and Transaero run safe international and domestic services.

4 Flight Deals

There are not many cheap flights from the West to St Petersburg, although once or twice a year, Aeroflot offers very good deals on flights to Moscow – check their website for details.

5 By Boat from Moscow

The journey by boat from Moscow takes around two weeks. Boats dock in St Petersburg at the River Terminal, near Proletarskaya metro station.

6 Arriving by Train from Moscow

There are many trains from Moscow to St Petersburg, including an express daytime train, which takes five hours. However, the most popular trains are the overnight ones, which take over eight hours. You can travel by *platzkarte*, *coupe* or SV, which are, respectively, a seat in a carriage, a berth in a four-person cabin and a bed in a two-person cabin. Most trains arrive at Ploshchad Vosstaniya.

7 Immigration Cards

All visitors are given an immigration card upon arrival. This must be kept on your person for the entire duration of the visit and shown to the police upon request. Photocopies are usually not accepted. You are required to carry your passport at all times, too.

8 Customs

If you are carrying cash over the value of US$1,500, antiques, valuable jewellery, laptops, or other electrical equipment upon entry into Russia, you will have to fill out a customs declaration form. You will need to present it when you leave, so that you can take the items back with you.

9 Taxis from the Airport

Taxis from the airport to the city can be booked in advance and cost about $50. You will also find official city taxis, which are not really any cheaper than pre-booked cars, and private taxis *(see p104)* which cost around $25 – make sure you agree on the fare beforehand.

🔟 Buses from the Airport

The Nos 13 and 39 buses leave for the city from Pulkovo 1 and Pulkovo 2 respectively. The "Airport Express" bus is also available every 15 minutes. The *marshrutnoye taksi* (minibuses) travel the same route, but are a lot faster and more comfortable, although slightly more expensive. They park near arrivals and leave when they are full.

Directory

Airports
• Pulkovo 1: Map G2; 704 3822
• Pulkovo 2: Map G2; 704 3444

Airlines
• Aeroflot: 438 5583; www.aeroflot.ru
• Transaero: 579 6463 / 1974; transaero.ru
• Rossiya Airlines: 333 2222; pulkovo.ru

Trains
• All train enquiries: call 055

Left **A taxi** Right **A bus on Vasilevskiy Island**

10 Getting Around

1 Metro
The city's metro is incredibly good value and trains come at fast intervals, ranging from a minute during rush hour, to four or five minutes late at night. The metro is open until midnight, although trains continue to run until 12:15am. More than just a mode of public transport, the metro is a sight in its own right *(see pp50–51)*.

2 Buses
While ticket prices are increasing rapidly, a bus journey is still good value. Bus stops are identifiable by their white and yellow signs with a red "A" (for *avtobus*). These buses can be very crowded during rush hour. The expensive, privately run buses add a "K" before their bus numbers, which are the same as those of the state-operated buses.

3 Trams
Trams (*tramvai*) are popular all over the former Soviet Union, and St Petersburg is no exception. The stops are identifiable by the red and white signs above the tram rails. Less crowded than buses, they are a great way to see the city. However, they tend to break down frequently.

4 Trolley Buses
Trolley buses, unlike trams, run up and down Nevskiy prospekt, and in this part of the city, at least, are a very convenient and cheap way of getting around. However, they can get uncomfortably crowded and, like trams, often break down. Blue and white signs mark the stops.

5 Taxis
Official, licensed taxis are very hard to find, but the number is steadily growing and it is now possible to order a taxi. Numbers for taxi firms can be found in most local newspapers. Licensed taxis are easier to find outside the top hotels, although their prices are, as you would imagine, a lot higher.

6 Walking
St Petersburg is an excellent city for walking. Many of the main sights, especially those at the city's centre, are extremely close together, making it easy to travel from one to the other by foot.

7 Street Signs
Street signs are in both Russian and English in the centre, but those in the outskirts of the city are in Russian only. The English street signs are a relatively recent phenomenon. Many were erected in time for the city's 300th anniversary *(see p33)*.

8 Mini Buses
Mini buses (*marshrutnoye taksi*) are privately run and sprang up in the years following *perestroika*, quickly becoming a feature of city life. They travel around the city, following standard bus routes. Pay the driver when you get in or take your seat and pass the money on. Be careful not to slam the door – for some reason the drivers particularly dislike this.

9 Chastniki
Chastniki are private taxi drivers who drive around the city looking for fares. Their cars are not designated as taxis – you need to put your hand out to attract one. In the days following the collapse of the USSR, many of the *chastniki* were newly impoverished scientists, lawyers and other professional people looking to make ends meet. Today they mostly tend to be pensioners, immigrants and students trying to earn a bit of cash on the side.

10 Tickets and Travel Cards
Yediniy Bileti are travel cards that cover all forms of transport and are available with a fortnightly or monthly validity period. Good value if you are staying for a long time, they can easily be bought at metro stations. All modes of transport run on a flat fare system. Regular tickets can be bought from conductors or drivers, and at ticket booths in the metro.

Official yellow taxis can be booked at reasonable rates by dialling 600 8888

Left **A raised bridge** Right **Fake Soviet memorabilia**

Things to Avoid

1 Tap Water
It is best to avoid the tap water here. Although the authorities claim it is safe, the pipes that carry it are old. It would be better to stick to bottled water, which is widely available. The tap water is fine for showers.

2 Over-drinking
Russians are famed for their drinking and usually drink their vodka straight, in a single gulp. If you decide to get into a drinking session with the locals, follow their example and take a bite to eat after each shot to soak up the alcohol – failure to do so can have dreadful consequences.

3 Getting into Taxis with Extra Passengers
When stopping a private car, make sure that there are no other passengers in it. Some gangs of robbers drive around the city, posing as *chastniki*. Make sure that the back seat is empty before getting into a car.

4 Gangs of Beggars
Gangs of beggars roam the main tourist areas. Many of them, usually children, can be very difficult to shake off if you give them money. The best thing, unfortunately, is just to ignore them. If you really want to hand over some cash, make absolutely sure they are alone.

5 Getting Stranded Due to Raised Bridges
During the summer, the city's many bridges are raised between 2–5am to allow ships to pass. This can lead to problems. It is easy to get stranded coming home late at night, particularly if you are staying on the outskirts of the city. Consult the website for details. ✆ http://www.st-petersburg.ru/en/transport/bridges

6 Police "Spot-checks"
The police supplement their meagre salaries by stopping passersby, demanding to see passports and registration documents. They often claim there is some "irregularity" – one that is usually non-existent – and demand payment of an on-the-spot fine, but no receipts are offered. If you are sure there is nothing wrong with your documents and do not want to pay $10–20, simply refuse and they will, eventually, go away. Of course, this works better if you speak Russian confidently.

7 Skinheads
In recent years, the city has gained a reputation as the centre of right-wing extremism in Russia. Skinhead gangs have been known to attack non-caucasian residents and visitors. To avoid any such incident, it is best not to linger at the metro at night and to be aware of your surroundings at all times. That said, however, the threat is exaggerated by the media and there is little point in getting unduly paranoid.

8 The "Dropped Wallet" Scam
One of the most popular cons starts with a wallet being dropped. When a helpful tourist picks it up, the person who dropped it, at first grateful, then accuses the tourist of having lifted some cash. The rest varies, almost always ending with the tourist out of pocket. Avoid dropped wallets like the plague!

9 Fake Soviet Memorabilia
The demand for Soviet memorabilia far outstrips the supply and many of the goods will have been produced especially for the tourist market.

10 "Bad" Vodka
Cheap, even poisonous, vodka has been a problem in Russia ever since Mikhail Gorbachev's "dry law" saw Russians mass-produce bootleg alcohol. There are many deaths every year due to drinking "bad" vodka. As a rule, the more expensive the vodka is, and the more respectable the shop, the more likely a bottle is to be safe and genuine.

Left **Shaking hands** Centre **Model of a ticket-seller displaying his "public front"** Right **Toasting**

⟨10⟩ Etiquette

1 Greetings
Men greet each other with a handshake. Women are greeted with a nod or, if they are very close, a kiss on the cheek. Friends of all ages greet each other with the word "Privet!", while "Zdravstvuyte" is used for formal occasions.

2 Political Discussions
Russians are, more by circumstance than by desire, accustomed to political discussion. While the younger generation is more politically apathetic than that which grew up in the USSR, discussions on the Chechen War can become heated, particularly if a tone critical of Russia's actions there is taken.

3 Personal Questions
Russians are a lot more willing to ask, and answer, questions that may be considered to be of a personal nature in the West. These may include questions about salaries or even family life. However, as a foreigner, you may be seen to be "prying" if you are the one who initiates such a bout of questioning!

4 Giving Up Seats
It is accepted practice for young men and women to give up seats to their elders, pregnant women and invalids on public transport. Failure

to do so may lead to on-the-spot public condemnation from your fellow passengers. The younger generation is, however, slowly losing the habit of public transport gallantry.

5 Male/Female Relations
In Russia, men are expected to foot the bill in restaurants for ladies. Any suggestion to go Dutch would be frowned upon. Also, Western women may be shocked or delighted, depending on their outlook, to find doors opened for them, to be helped off buses and to be excluded from any physical work.

6 Drinking and Customs
Russians drink plenty of vodka and the process of drinking has its own rituals. Never drink from the bottle and always take a bite to eat between shots *(see p103)*. Toasts are long and frequently made – if you are called upon to make one, a simple "Za Zdorovie!" ("to your health!") just won't be enough.

7 Smoking
Russians are among the world's heaviest smokers. Most restaurants have a section set aside for them. There are no smoke-free bars or clubs. However, smoking is banned on public transport. Cigarettes are cheap in Russia, with

many foreign brands being bootlegged. There are also the Russian non-filtered cigarettes on sale for absurdly cheap prices

8 Being A Guest
If you are invited to a private flat, it is customary to bring a bottle of something, and some flowers for the woman of the house. Russians take their shoes off at home and change into slippers.

9 The "Public Front"
In offices, shops and stations, there is a "public front" which involves a certain rudeness when dealing with strangers, although attitudes are changing. These same people may well be warm, kind individuals. However, if you are encountering them in their guise of minor official, shop assistant or ticket-seller, you are not likely to experience the benign side of their character.

10 In Churches
Orthodox churches are intense places where mankind is made to feel its utter powerlessness. There are no pews – worshippers stand for entire services. Women cover their heads while men remove their hats. Photography is allowed for a fee in some churches, but may be strictly forbidden in others. Candles, sold at most churches, can be placed in front of the icons.

Left **A street food stall** Centre **A** *zakuski* **spread** Right **A menu in Russian**

TOP 10 Dining in St Petersburg

1 Street Food
Street food is found in abundance, from ice-cream and hot dogs to pies and doner kebabs. While most of it is safe to eat, some meat products, especially those sold by old women around the main train terminals, should probably be avoided – the "meat" may be of dubious origin.

2 Tipping
Tipping is not expected in taxis, but is commonplace in restaurants. At places where it is not included in a service charge, feel free to leave as much as you consider right – 10–15 per cent is the norm.

3 Restaurant Opening Hours
Most restaurants and cafés open around noon. Many stay open until the last guest leaves while some close their doors from around 11pm. In top-end hotels, restaurants open for breakfast, as do many cafés in the city. Alcohol can be bought round the clock.

4 Zakuski
Zakuski (appetisers), are usually eaten cold before the main meal. These could be salads, marinated mushrooms, pancakes, pickled herring or gherkins. They are usually served with bread and sour cream. There are also specific *zakuski* to accompany beer and vodka, including dried, salted fish, dried squid and anchovies.

5 Menus
In a majority of the restaurants in the centre and other tourist areas, menus will be in Russian and English. However, outside these areas, they are likely to be in Russian only, and it is improbable that your waiter will know more than a few words of English. In this case, make good use of the phrasebook at the back of this book *(see pp126–8)*.

6 Restaurant Areas
The main restaurant area is Nevskiy prospekt and the streets around it. Here, you can find a wide selection of cuisines, from Japanese to Georgian. Once you get outside this area, however, restaurants become thinner on the ground. The area around the Mariinskiy Theatre *(see pp16–17)* is also good for restaurants and cafés.

7 Sushi
Sushi is wildly popular all over Russia. In fact, according to a recent survey, Russia boasts the most sushi restaurants in the world outside of Japan. The quality, however, varies, from freshly flown-in to deep-frozen lumps of "fish". As always, let the price and reputation of the eatery be your guide.

8 Attracting the Attention of Waiters/Waitresses
The Russian for waiter and waitress is *"ofitsant"* and *"ofitsantka"*, respectively. Yet it is customary to attract the attention of waitresses with a simple *"Devushka!"* (Girl!). It may sound very rude in the translation, but no one takes offence.

9 Vegetarian Options
In the USSR, vegetarianism was practically non-existent. However, since the collapse of the Soviet system, more and more Russians have begun to give up meat. Their numbers are still small, so there are only a few vegetarian restaurants in Russia, and practically none outside St Petersburg. The good news for vegetarians in St Petersburg is Idiot *(see p70)*, which serves non-meat versions of traditional Russian dishes.

10 Caucasian Food
Caucasian food hails from the former Soviet republics of Georgia, Armenia and Azerbaijan. Ranging from doner-kebab-type *"shashlik"* to the spicy, often meat-free dishes of Georgia, this cuisine is very popular all over Russia. The excellent red wine from Georgia is currently in limited supply due to a bitter political quarrel between the neighbours.

Left **Russian roubles** Centre **A local postbox** Right **An Internet café sign**

Banking and Communications

Currency
The currency of Russia is the rouble. One rouble consists of 100 kopeks. The rouble has stabilized of late, but the currency cannot be obtained outside Russia even today. A few years ago, many businesses gave prices in US dollars, or Y.E. (a dollar equivalent). While this is still common, many are switching over to indicating prices in roubles.

Changing Money
Exchange booths are freely available all over the city these days. US dollars and Euros are the easiest to change, while pounds sterling can be changed in banks and top hotels. Avoid anyone who offers to change money for you on the street – he is certainly a swindler.

Credit Cards
Major credit cards are readily accepted at all top restaurants and hotels, but not at most other places, such as small shops and cafés. The widely accepted credit cards are Eurocard, VISA and MasterCard; American Express is not as recognized. If your credit card is lost or stolen, immediately inform the credit card company.

Traveller's Cheques
Traveller's cheques have not really caught on in Russia and are only accepted in a handful of banks. Commission is generally 3 per cent. The American Express traveller's cheques can be cashed at American Express offices for a commission of 2 per cent – you will need to provide your passport as proof of identity.

Post
Post out of Russia can be incredibly slow and unreliable – letters to the US or Europe can take months to arrive, or even longer. Westpost runs a reliable, fairly inexpensive service. The Corinthia Nevskij Palace Hotel *(see p62)* operates a good postal service via Finland. This service is of European standards and letters to the UK take three to four days to arrive. ✪ *Map E4 • Nevskiy prospekt 86 • 275 0784 • Open 9:30am–8pm Mon–Fri, noon–8pm Sat–Sun • www.westpost.ru*

Telephones
There are many public telephones in St Petersburg. While some accept coins, the majority only take telephone cards. These cards are sold at metro underpasses and at some of the metro ticket offices. Calls are relatively cheap.

Calling St Petersburg
In order to call Russia from abroad, dial 007. To reach a number within the city, dial 007 and then the city code – 812 – followed by the number you are trying to reach. To dial Moscow from St Petersburg, or vice versa, dial 8 and wait for the dial tone. Then dial the number, beginning with the respective city code.

Mobiles
Most of the mobile phones with the roaming facility will work here, but the service is very expensive. To be sure, check with your provider before leaving. If you are in Russia for some time, it makes sense to buy a SIM card from one of the local providers.

Internet Cafés
Internet cafés can be found all over the city, especially at the centre, on and around Nevskiy prospekt. They are identifiable by the word "Internet" in English. Speeds are fast and cheap.

ATMs
ATMs are easy to find throughout St Petersburg. They usually have an English language option. Cash can be obtained with a credit card through the larger banks. Commission is from 2 to 5 per cent. There are limits on the amount of cash that can be withdrawn in a single 24-hour period – these vary from bank to bank. Be careful when counting out your money in public.

Left **Beware of pickpockets** Centre **A police car** Right **An *apteka* (pharmacy)**

Security and Health

Crime

Petty crime, like in any big city, is common, but organized crime, in the form of the Russian Mafia, is unlikely to affect the average tourist.

Emergency

In an emergency, 02 is the official emergency hotline, but the operator may not speak English. There is a police hotline for foreigners. You may also want to consider contacting your consulate if you have a particularly serious problem.

Personal Safety

As in any large city, take all the precautions that you normally would to protect yourself. Avoid walking alone at night and keep your passport in a safe place. Watch out for scams, but try not to be paranoid. Women tourists need not feel unsafe, but it is best to avoid travelling alone by cab late at night.

Pickpocketing

The pickpocket gangs work the main tourist areas – Nevskiy prospekt is a favourite haunt. Be careful on the metro – watch out for wandering hands and people pressing up close to you. If you can, leave your valuables in the hotel safe.

Police

There are different sorts of police in St Petersburg. Firstly, there are the beat cops, or *militsya*, who wear dark blue-grey uniforms. There is also the OMON, who deal with special situations, including football hooligans and demonstrations. They are identifiable by their badges and grim demeanours. Lastly, there are the traffic cops, or DPS. The police are notorious for stopping drivers and extracting "fines" for minor infringements of the law.

Hospitals

If you become ill, and are staying at a good hotel, speak to someone at reception or dial the number for ambulances. However, the service is slow and the operator is unlikely to speak English. The MEDEM Clinic specializes in dealing with foreigners. If you have minor cuts or bruises, it would be cheaper to go to the Trauma Clinic of the Central District.

Pharmacies

The word for pharmacy is *apteka*. These are very easy to find, with many of them open 24 hours. However, it is a good idea to bring essential medicines with you, as they may be known under different names at the local pharmacies.

Dentists

Good dentistry is expensive. The MEDEM clinic provides dentistry services, but they are not cheap. An alternative is to ask your hotel to provide you with an English-speaking dentist.

Embassies and Consulates

If you lose your passport or are robbed, promptly contact your consulate or embassy. Note that embassies and consulates are extremely reluctant to lend money, though. The UK, US, Canada and Australia consulates are in St Petersburg, while Ireland's and New Zealand's are in Moscow.

Racism

An all-prevalent, casual racism is fairly deeply ingrained into Russian society. While much of it is directed at Chechens and other members of the southern republics, non-caucasian visitors may find themselves being stared at. However, the situation is improving as the younger generation is exposed to various ethnic groups.

Directory

Emergency
• Hotline: 02; 578 3014
• Ambulance: 03

Medical Services
• MEDEM Clinic: Map D6; Ulitsa Marata 6; 336 3333; www.medem.ru
• Trauma Clinic of the Central District: Map M3; Malaya Konyushennaya 2; 571 4396

Left **Budget hotels cater to backpackers** Centre **A hotel's "stars"** Right **Hotel taxis**

Accommodation Tips

Areas
The main five-star hotels are located in the centre, on and around Nevskiy prospekt. There are some good hotels further out as well. Budget hotels, catering to students and young people, have also begun to spring up in the last few years. Most of them, again, are located in and around the city centre.

Hotel Standards
Top quality, international chain hotels will have impeccably clean rooms, efficient service and be of the expected standard. Other hotels can be something of a hit-and-miss affair. Generally, however, all hotels are clean and the staff is polite, though language may be a problem.

Star System
The hotel star system in Russia is somewhat arbitrary, with many hotels awarding themselves the number of stars they feel they deserve. Keep in mind that the overall standard of hotels is lower than it is in the West. However, five-star hotels, particularly those with an international reputation, will always meet the equivalent global standards.

Booking
If you are thinking of a visit during the peak White Nights period, it is wise to book a room a few months in advance. Most hotels now have an online booking system. There are also agencies that provide booking services. The top hotels can also provide visa support for short stays.

Hidden Charges
Some hotels fail to include taxes or breakfast in the advertised price. This can come as something of a shock when checking out, so be sure to ask. Making phone calls from your room, especially international ones, is very expensive. In smaller hotels, local calls may be free, while the international line will probably be locked.

Payment
Payments can be made in the top hotels by credit card or cash. In smaller hotels, cash may be your only option. Larger hotels may require credit card details to make bookings, with money debited in the event of a late cancellation. Hotel prices go up significantly during the White Nights period.

Children
While all hotels welcome families, only a few have children's facilities. The large chain hotels offer certain services and may help arrange a babysitter for you – check this before booking. Some of the restaurants have special children's menus.

Hotel Taxis
Taxis provided by your hotel are more expensive than the usual taxis or the *chastniki (see p104)*. However, they do have the advantage of being very safe, with cars that are in good condition. If you can afford it, take a hotel taxi. If not, be careful when dealing with *chastniki*.

Security
Again, the top hotels are the safest, with security guards, regular bag searches and metal detectors. However, it is still a good idea to leave your valuables in the hotel's safe. Smaller hotels may simply have a doorman, who, in some places, may even be a moonlighting member of the city's police force. Generally, hotels are safe in the city, although you need to exercise basic precautionary measures.

Private Flats
Private flats are often a good alternative to hotels, especially if you are going to be staying in the city for some time. There are a few options. The cheapest, but not the safest, is to approach the old women who meet the trains from Moscow at Moskovskiy Vokzal. However, these flats, while a lot cheaper, are something of a hit-and-miss option. Alternatively, try a private firm *(see p115)*.

  ***Note**: Unless otherwise stated, all hotels accept credit cards, have ensuite bathrooms and air conditioning*

Left **Cheap local beers** Centre **A local shopping mall** Right **One of St Petersburg's boutiques**

🔟 Shopping Tips

1 Opening Hours
Most of the shops are usually open from 10am until 7pm, seven days a week. The city has many 24-hour shops, ranging from simple grocery stores to hip boutiques.

2 Credit Cards
Only top places accept credit cards. Some shops may advertise the fact that they accept cards, but this is a *perestroika*-period hangover from when stickers advertising Western goods and services were stuck up even if not actually offered. Carry plenty of cash when shopping. You may be asked to show your passport when paying by credit card.

3 Haggling
Haggling is not practised in shops, but in markets, especially the ones selling souvenirs, it is expected. Do not expect huge discounts, as the price you are offered is probably about 15 per cent more than the minimum the stall owner is willing to accept. If you are buying in bulk, discounts can be higher.

4 Refunds
Refunds in Russia are given only if you have the *chek* (original receipt). However, for electronic items, you may be directed to the manufacturing company's local service centre. The law on refunds is subject to change, but if you can read Russian, the most recent version of the law is usually displayed on the shop's noticeboard.

5 Shopping Areas
St Petersburg's main shopping areas are located around the commercial part of Gostinyy Dvor, but the items here are most expensive. Apart from goods such as vodka and caviar, the city is not exactly a shoppers' paradise – prices for a great deal of goods are likely to be even higher than in the West.

6 DVDs and CDs
Although the government makes noises about clamping down on illegal DVDs and CDs, Russia, along with China and the neighbouring Ukraine, remains one of the biggest producers of bootleg films, music and software in the world. Pirate DVDs are available all over St Petersburg for about $4 a film. Quality, however, may not always be good.

7 Shopping for Clothes
Russians, especially women, are extremely fashion conscious – a reaction to the severe lack of choice during the Soviet period. Imported clothes, especially the designer labels at St Petersburg's boutiques, are very expensive.

8 Electronics
There are no bargains to be had in Russia when it comes to electronic items, such as music systems and DVD players. Many of these items will be a lot more expensive than in the West – the result of a severe lack of competitive pricing on the domestic market. Indeed, many Russians bring electronic items home with them from their trips abroad.

9 Alcohol
Although a law has recently been passed forbidding the sale of drinks with an alcohol content of over 15 per cent between 11pm–8am, strong liquor is, nevertheless, very easy to come by. Alcohol is absurdly cheap, and even Soviet champagne *(see p37)* goes for less than $10 a bottle. Imported beer in bars is the only exception, costing the same or even more than it would in the West.

10 Buying Food
There are lots of supermarkets and grocery stores in the city, many of them now open round the clock. Prices in St Petersburg are generally cheaper than in Moscow. Vegetables are more expensive during winter, when they have to be imported. Bread is subsidized by the government and is of a very good quality.

Left **The Astoria** Centre **Grand Hotel Europe** Right **Radisson SAS Royal Hotel**

TOP 10 Luxury Hotels

1 Astoria
The Astoria Hotel enjoys an excellent location in a quiet area of the city. Fully renovated in 2002, the hotel's front rooms offer wonderful views of St Isaac's Square and the Moyka river. The hotel also boasts a nightclub, good restaurants and a fitness centre. ✆ Map K4
• Bolshaya Morskaya ulitsa 39 • 494 5757 • www.thehotel astoria.com • $$$$$

2 Grand Hotel Europe
The Grand Hotel Europe's historic interiors and fine restaurants make it one of the city's very best. Established more than a century ago, the hotel is an institution that has consistently boasted high standards. ✆ Map N3
• Mikhaylovskaya ulitsa 1/7 • 329 6000 • www.grand hoteleurope.com • $$$$$

3 Kempinski Hotel Moika
This hotel opened in 2005 and has since become one of the city's most popular upmarket hotels. It is part of a German chain and has a splendid restaurant with great views. ✆ Map M3
• Nab. reki Moyki 22 • 335 9111 • www.kempinksi.com • $$$$$

4 Renaissance St Petersburg Baltic
An atmospheric hotel in one of the city's oldest areas, the Renaissance is a luxury hotel with character. Part of the worldwide Marriott chain, it contains a good fitness club and an excellent restaurant. ✆ Map J4
• Pochtamtskaya ulitsa 4 • 380 4000 • www.marriott. com • $$$$$

5 Eliseev Palace
This recently renovated luxury hotel, part of the Taleon Club, has an on-site casino. It is one of the few hotels in the city to arrange events for children, and every guest is given their own personal valet. The rooms overlook the Moyka river. ✆ Map M2
• Nab. reki Moyki 59 • 324 9911 • www.eliseev palacehotel.com • $$$$$

6 Corinthia Nevskij Palace Hotel
Ideally located, this hotel has a range of superb restaurants and shops. The Imperial restaurant here serves a great Sunday brunch that is also open to non-guests. Rooms are bright and spacious, and service is friendly and efficient. ✆ Map E4 • Nevskiy prospekt 57 • 380 2001 • www. corinthiahotels.com • $$$$$

7 Grand Hotel Emerald
This fine, top-end hotel contains a fitness centre and a large sauna. There are a number of high-quality restaurants and the hotel's large rooms are comfortable. While not as centrally located as other five-star hotels, the Grand Hotel Emerald is well served by public transport. ✆ Map F4
• Suvorovskiy prospekt 18 • 740 5000 • www.grand hotelemerald.com • $$$$$

8 Radisson SAS Royal Hotel
This hotel, part of the well-known international hotel chain and very close to major sights, offers free broadband, a fitness centre and top quality service. Its cafés and rooms have great views of Nevskiy prospekt. ✆ Map E4
• Nevskiy prospekt 49/2 • 322 5000 • www. radissonsas.com • $$$$$

9 Baltic Star Hotel
This five-star hotel is popular with visiting officials. It offers 18 VIP cottages (which really are two-storey houses with professional chefs), private parking and views of the nearby Gulf of Finland. The hotel's regular rooms are also of the highest standards. ✆ Map G1 • Berezovaya alleya 3 • 438 5700 • www. balticstar-hotel.ru • $$$$$

10 Novotel
Ideal for disabled visitors, with especially adapted rooms, this hotel is very modern in design and features a superb restaurant. ✆ Map E4
• Mayakovskovo ulitsa 3a • 335 1188 • www.novotel. spb.ru • $$$$$

 Note: Unless otherwise stated, all hotels accept credit cards, have ensuite bathrooms and air conditioning

Price Categories

For a double room per night, including taxes and breakfast, during the high season. In the low season, prices can halve.

US$	Under $100
US$$	$100–$175
US$$$	$175–$250
US$$$$	$250–$325
US$$$$$	over $325

The Fifth Corner Business Hotel's interiors

🏆10 Business and Top-End Hotels

1 Petro Palace
Petro Palace opened its doors in 2005, instantly becoming popular with wealthier Russians on holiday or business trips. Housed in a renovated 19th-century building, the hotel offers a fitness centre and a pool. 🕭 *Map L3 • Malaya Morskaya ulitsa 14 • 571 2880 • www.petro palacehotel.com • $$$$$*

2 Hotel Dostoevsky
Housed in a 24-hour shopping mall, this modern hotel is within walking distance of many of St Petersburg's top sights. It has a sauna and a fitness centre, and the shopping mall is full of everything you could possibly need. 🕭 *Map E5 • Vladimirskiy prospekt 19 • 331 3200 • www. dostoevsky-hotel.ru • $$$$*

3 Helvetia Hotel & Suites
The Helvetia is located some distance from the main tourist area, but is still within comfortable walking distance from the major sights. Set in a quiet courtyard, the staff is friendly and the rooms are comfortable – some have their own kitchen equipment. 🕭 *Map E5 • Ulitsa Marata 11 • 326 5353 • www.helvetia-suites.ru • $$$$*

4 Fifth Corner Business Hotel
The Fifth Corner Hotel, *Pyatiy Ugol* in Russian, is specifically aimed at business people and has conference facilities. It also functions as a fine tourist hotel, with fair-sized rooms and views of the street. It has a fusion restaurant and is not far from Nevskiy prospekt. 🕭 *Map P5 • Zagorodnyy prospekt 13 • 380 8181 • www.5ugol.ru • $$$*

5 Karelia Business Hotel
This modern business hotel is a short taxi ride away from the main sights. It is good value for money, making it a great option for the frugal tourist – a buffet breakfast is included in the price. 🕭 *Map H1 • Malaya Tukhachevskogo 27/2 • 718 40 48 • www. karelia.spb.ru • $$$*

6 Pulkovskaya
Not far from the airport, Pulkovskaya is convenient for day trips to Pavlovsk and Tsarskoe Selo. Boasting its own bakery and brewery, the hotel is a good place for those wishing to explore the city's environs. 🕭 *Map G2 • Pobedy ploshchad 1 • 740 3900 • www. rezidorparkinn.com • $$$*

7 Pribaltiyskaya
This modernized Soviet colossus is away from the city centre; the nearest metro is also at a distance. However, it is perfect for walks along the Gulf of Finland, has a pool and offers business facilities. Be sure to ask for a room with a relaxing view of the gulf when booking in. 🕭 *Korablestroiteley ulitsa 14 • 329 2626 • www. hotelpribaltiyskaya.ru • $$$*

8 Ermitage Hotel
This four-star hotel has all of four rooms! It is ideal for large groups – the hoteliers point out that the entire place can be booked. It makes for a comfortable stay and is only a few minutes away from The Hermitage. 🕭 *Map M2 • Millonnaya ulitsa 11 • 571 5497 • www. ermitage.spb.ru • $$$*

9 Caso Leto
The rooms of this family-run hotel are large and it is close to the top sights in the city. Guests get free Internet access as well as some complimentary international calls. The staff is helpful and also provides visa support. 🕭 *Map C4 • Bolshaya Morskaya ulitsa 34 • 600 1096 • www. casaleto.com • $$$*

10 Alexander House Club
This hotel takes real pride in its spacious and elegant rooms – two luxury suites even boast working fireplaces. Reconstructed in the style of a 19th-century gentleman's house, the hotel also has a small bar and restaurant. 🕭 *Map J6 • Nab. Kryukova Kanala 27 • 575 3877 • www.a-house. ru • $$$*

Left **The St Petersburg** Centre **Polikoff's interiors** Right **Tavricheskaya Hotel**

Mid-Range Hotels

1 Prestige Hotel Center
A modest hotel close to the Admiralty Gardens. It offers simple rooms with showers. The furniture is basic but functional, and the staff is friendly. ⊗ Map N6 • Gorokhovaya ulitsa 5 • 312 0405 • www.prestige-hotels.com • $$

2 Polikoff
A comfortable but unspectacular hotel. The rooms overlook a quiet courtyard. Clean and functional is the order of the day here. The staff is friendly. The hoteliers also run a sideline business in the renting out of luxury limousines, which is surprisingly cheap. ⊗ Map P4 • Karavannaya ulitsa 11/64 • 995 3488 • www.polikoff.ru • $$

3 Azimut Hotel
The glitzy Azimut is unexpectedly cheap, and is a taxi ride or a tram journey away from the major sights. There is a wide range of rooms available here. ⊗ Map B5 • Lermontovskiy prospekt 43/1 • 740 2640 • http:// eng.azimuthotels.ru • $$

4 Rossiya
Set amongst the Stalinist buildings of Moskovskiy prospekt, the Rossiya Hotel is great value, even if it is some distance away from the city centre. The area is well-served by public transport. Popular with Russians visiting the city

as well as tourists, the hotel has a restaurant and a bar. ⊗ Chernyshevskovo ploshchad 11 • 329 3932 • www.rossiya-hotel.ru • $$

5 Matisov Domik
A cosy, three-star hotel overlooking a tree-lined waterway, Matsiov Domik is popular with many famous Russian actors. Despite being badly served by public transport, guests can take a taxi or a long walk to the centre of town. The hotel also has its own small, but fine, restaurant. ⊗ Map A5 • Nab. reki Pryazhki 3 /1 • 495 1439 • www.matisov. spb.ru • $$

6 St Petersburg
The St Petersburg is another hotel that is perfectly functional, but a little isolated. It does, however, have fabulous views of the city's embankments from the rooms on the south side. The rooms are clean and comfortable. ⊗ Map E2 • Pirogovskaya nab. 5 / 2 • 380 1919 • www.hotel-spb.ru • $$

7 Okhtinskaya
The Okhtinskaya is a little out of the way, but the hotel runs shuttle buses to Nevskiy prospekt. There is a danger of being cut off in summer when the bridges are raised, so guests should be aware of the timings for this (see

p105). The building is modern and the rooms are fairly spacious. ⊗ Map G2 • Bolsheokhtinskiy prospekt 4 • 227 4438 • www.okhtinskaya.com • $$

8 LDM
Not exactly central, the LDM is, nevertheless, a fine hotel for those on a budget. Built in 1975, it is located in an "ecologically clean area of the city". It has clean, functional rooms and is popular with visiting Russians. ⊗ Map B1 • Ulitsa Professora Popova 47 • 234 3278 • www.ldm. ru • $$

9 Stony Island Hotel
A good, modern hotel, but a little way out from the centre. However, it offers good value and the rooms are all well equipped. It has a laundry service, and a restaurant-bar serving American and European cuisine. ⊗ Map C1 • Kamennoostrovskiy prospekt 45 • 337 2434 • www.stonyisland.ru • $$

10 Tavricheskaya Hotel
This is a no-frills hotel – strictly not for those seeking comfort. However, its location makes it a great base for sight-seeing, especially for those on a budget. The rooms are clean and functional, and the staff is friendly. ⊗ Map G2 • Shpalernaya ulitsa 55 • 716 4550 • $$

Streetsmart

Note: Unless otherwise stated, all hotels accept credit cards, have ensuite bathrooms and air conditioning

Price Categories

For a double room per night, including taxes and breakfast, during the high season. In the low season, prices can halve.

US$	Under $100
US$$	$100–$175
US$$$	$175–$250
US$$$$	$250–$325
US$$$$$	over $325

Left **St Petersburg International Youth Hostel's entrance** Right **A room at Vesta**

Budget Options

Vesta
Vesta is set in a green courtyard just off Nevskiy prospekt. The rooms are clean, the staff friendly and the location excellent. ⌖ *Map E4 • Nevskiy prospekt 92 • 272 1322 • www.vesta hotel.spb.ru • $$*

German Club
This established "mini-hotel" is within comfortable walking distance of Moskovskaya metro station. The staff is friendly and the rooms are very simple, yet cosy. The "Lux-Room" option is very comfortable and great value too. ⌖ *Map G1 • Gastello ulitsa 20 • 371 5104 • www.hotel germanclub.com • $*

Mir
This 1970s budget hotel has huge double rooms with showers and phones. It offers cheap sharing options and has a restaurant that serves traditional Russian food on the premises. ⌖ *Map G1 • Gastello ulitsa 17 • 708 5166 • www. hotelmir.spb.ru • $*

Private Flats
Private flats vary from luxurious, multi-roomed affairs in the very centre of the city to one-room dumps in the suburbs. Private agencies *(see website)* offer good deals, but you may have to book early during White Nights *(see p102)* and other peak times.

Flats rented through a private firm will generally be clean and secure. ⌖ *www.spb-rentals.com • Prices can vary wildly*

St Petersburg International Youth Hostel
Close to many of the major sights, this hostel offers very basic, yet clean, rooms. It also provides visa support and, as their site boasts, the chance to meet other "cool people" to see the city with. ⌖ *Map F4 • 3-ya Sovestskaya 28 • 329 8018 • www.ryh.ru • $*

Retur Camping
Camping is not really very popular in Russia – official campsites are rare and located some way from the city. The Retur campsite, while offering some actual camping, is in reality more of a campsite-cum-motel located next to the Gulf of Finland. It is good for a relaxing holiday, although somewhat inconvenient for sight-seeing. ⌖ *Primorskoye schosse 202 • 437 7533 • www.retur.ru/engl/engl.htm • $*

Sleep Cheap
Sleep Cheap allows you to do exactly what it says. Located close to the city centre, the hostel is a good option. Again, no frills, but the rooms are clean and safe. It also offers an apartment for rent,

which, although a way out, is cheap. Breakfast is included in the price. ⌖ *Map E3 • Mokhovaya ulitsa 18 • 715 1304 • www.sleepcheap.spb.ru • $*

All Seasons Hostel
This hostel offers dormitories as well as private rooms. Prices are cheap, especially in the off-season period. The hostel offers visa support. ⌖ *Map G1 • Yakovlevskiy pereulok 11 • 327 1070 • www.hostel.ru • $*

Yuzhnaya
There is a wide range of rooms here. They are not luxurious, but adequate enough. The cheapest rooms are singles and doubles with shared conveniences – the most expensive are the double-sized rooms with all the necessary facilities. ⌖ *Map E6 • Rasstannaya ulitsa 26 • 223 4643 • ww.ugnaya.ru • $–$$$*

Gelios
Gelios is located at a distance from the city, on the coast of the Gulf of Finland. It offers a spa centre with all manner of treatments. Not really for those looking to explore the city, the hotel is, nevertheless, a good option for a relaxing holiday with a day trip or two into the city. ⌖ *Map G1 • Primorskoye schosse 593 • 702 2626 • www.gelios-otel.ru • $$*

Left **Brothers Karamazov** Centre **Neva** Right **Oktiabrskaya**

TOP 10 Historic Hotels

1 Na Sadovoy
Na Sadovoy is located in the heart of Sennaya ploshchad. Its rooms range from dormitories to private rooms – some are without bathrooms. ◎ Map M5 • 53 Sadovaya ulitsa, 4th floor • 314 8357 • www.budget-travel.spb.ru • $

2 Angleterre
This upmarket hotel is famous for being the planned venue for the Nazi's "Victory Ball" scheduled to take place after the fall of the city during WWII – fortunately, the city never capitulated. The rooms here are comfortable. ◎ Map K4 • Bolshaya Morskaya ulitsa 39 • 494 5666 • www.angleterrehotel.com • $$$$$

3 Hotel Marshal
Located in a splendid 19th-century building, Hotel Marshal houses a museum devoted to the Finnish General Marshall Mannerheim that examines the 1939–41 Soviet-Finnish War. The hotel rooms are simply furnished, but cosy. ◎ Map F2 • Shpalernaya ulitsa 41 • 579 9955 • www.marshalhotel.spb.ru • $$

4 Brothers Karamazov
A must for Dostoevsky enthusiasts, the Brothers Karamazov is located close to the museum dedicated to the writer's life (see p34). Opened in 2004, each room is named after a female character in one of his works. The rooms are good-value and the staff is friendly. ◎ Map D5 • Sotsialisticheskaya ulitsa 11a • 335 1185 • www.karamazovhotel.ru • $$$

5 Oktiabrskaya
This is a renovated Soviet colossus with a Cold War-era atmosphere. Opened in 1851, it was famed for its state-of-the-art technology. The rooms are simple, clean and functional. ◎ Map E4 • Ligovskiy prospekt 10 • 578 1144 • www.oktoberhotel.spb.ru • $$

6 Neva
This pre-revolutionary hotel with a splendid façade opened in 1913 and operated throughout the Soviet era. Recently renovated, it still boasts an Imperial charm. It has a pool and a sauna, and offers a wide range of reasonably priced rooms. ◎ Map E3 • Chaykovskovo ulitsa 17 • 578 0504/05 • www.nevahotel.spb.ru • $$

7 Moskva
The cavernous Moskva, once a state-run Intourist hotel, has a distinctly old-fashioned feel about it. The service tends to be somewhat slow at times. Its rooms are clean and the very definition of functional. ◎ Map G5 • Aleksandra Nevskogo ploshchad 2 • 333 2444 • www.hotelmoscow.ru • $$$

8 Prestige Hotel
This hotel is housed in a 19th-century building just a short walk away from the Strelka and the Rostral Columns (see p82). The rooms are modern and comfortable. Both breakfast and, more importantly, visa support, are included in the price. ◎ Map A3 • 3-ya liniya 52 • 328 5011 • www.prestigehotels.com • $$

9 Domik V Kolomne
A cheap, comfortable hotel located by the Griboedov Canal, Domik V Kolomne prides itself on the fact that Pushkin (see p34) wrote many of his famous works during his stay here between 1816–8. The hotel is a genuine architectural treasure, unaltered from the 19th century. Rooms are a little on the gaudy side, with shower cabins in most of them rather than baths. ◎ Map A6 • Nab. kanala Griboedova 174a • 710 8351 • http://domikvkolomne.ru • $

10 Antique Hotel
Housed in the former residence of the Russian composer Rachmaninov, this hotel is furnished with antique furniture. Surprisingly good value, it is located close to the major sights. The hotel has a garden gallery that contains temporary exhibitions. ◎ Map M4 • Kazanskaya ulitsa 5 • 327 7466 • www.hotelrachmaninov.com • $$

Price Categories

For a double room per night, including taxes and breakfast, during the high season. In the low season, prices can halve.

US$	Under $100
US$$	$100–$175
US$$$	$175–$250
US$$$$	$250–$325
US$$$$$	over $325

A room at the Puppet Theatre Hostel

Hotels Handy for the Sights

1 Premiere
The Premiere is located "a stone's throw away" from the Mariinskiy Theatre *(see pp16–17)*. Inexpensive and comfortable, the rooms here are clean. ✆ *Map B5 • Ulitsa Soyuza Pechatnikov 4 • 714 1877 • www.spbhotel.com • $$*

2 Natali
This private hotel, although quite a distance from the city centre, is close to Tsarskoe Selo's palace and gardens *(see pp26–7)* and is ideal for a night or two out of the city. It is modern and has a round-the-clock bar. It does not offer visa support. ✆ *Malaya ulitsa 56a • 466 2913 • www. hotelnatali.spb.ru • $$*

3 Comfort
Comfort is a real find – an inexpensive hotel right in the centre of the city, close to many of the main sights, with rooms that are simple yet comfortable. ✆ *Map K4 • Bolshaya Morskaya ulitsa 25 • 570 6700 • www.comfort-hotel.spb.ru • $$*

4 Nevskiy
A three-star hotel right in the historic centre of St Petersburg, Nevskiy, with its range of comfortable rooms, is for those looking for a bit of luxury at affordable rates. ✆ *Map M3 • Bolshaya Konyushennaya ulitsa 10 • 703 3860 • www.hon.ru • $$$*

5 Kronverk
Superbly located for the Peter and Paul Fortress *(see pp20–21)*, Kronverk is situated in a business district. The rooms are pleasant and functional. Those who wish to stay in the city for a bit longer can book the hotel's flats. The city centre is a short, picturesque, stroll away. ✆ *Map B2 • Blokhina ulitsa 9 • 703 3663 • www. kronverk.com • $$*

6 Pushka Inn
Close to the Hermitage *(see pp10–13)*, Pushka (Cannon) Inn is housed in an 18th-century building near the Moyka river. Featuring friendly, English-speaking staff and a good, on-the-premises restaurant, the hotel is a fine medium-range choice at the heart of the city's historical centre. ✆ *Map M2 • Nab. reki Moyki 14 • 312 0913 • www. pushkainn.ru • $$$*

7 Arbat Nord
Originally intended to cater to business people, the Arbat Nord now also attracts tourists, thanks to its prime location close to the Field of Mars *(see p68)*. Rooms are stylish and equipped with all amenities. The hotel's European-style restaurant has a very good wine list. ✆ *Map E3 • Artilleriskaya ulitsa 4 • 703 1899 • www.arbat-nord.ru • $$$*

8 Puppet Theatre Hostel
A very cheap and friendly hostel right in the centre of the city, the Puppet Theatre Hostel is great for budget travellers. Located near ploshchad Vosstaniya, it is just a short walk to Nevskiy prospekt. The hotel has private rooms as well as shared dormitories, and offers visa support. ✆ *Map E3 • Nekrasova ulitsa 14 • 272 5401 • www. hostel-puppet.ru • $*

9 Hotel Shelfort
Perfectly located for exploring the Strelka area of Vasilevskiy Island *(see pp82–5)*, the hotel has a mere 15 rooms. For a cheap, no frills option situated within walking distance of the island's many sights, Hotel Shelfort, with its friendly staff, is ideal. ✆ *Map A3 • 3-ya liniya 26 • 328 0555 • www.shelfort.ru • $$*

10 Universitet Hotel
Once a government-owned hostel for students, the Universitet Hotel boasts a splendid location, right off Nevskiy prospekt, behind the Cathedral of Our Lady of Kazan *(see p8)*. It offers very cheap and extremely simple accommodation, and is popular with students from China, Korea and Vietnam. Advance bookings are not accepted. ✆ *Map M4 • Kazanskaya ulitsa 6 • 314 7472 • $*

General Index

Index

Acknowledgements

Author

MARC BENNETTS was born in London, UK and moved to St Petersburg in 1997, where he learnt Russian. Marc also contributed to DK's Eyewitness Guide to St Petersburg. He now lives in Moscow, not far from Red Square.

AT DORLING KINDERSLEY

Publisher
Douglas Amrine

List Manager
Christine Stroyan

Senior Editor
Sadie Smith

Project Editor
Alexandra Farrell

Design Manager
Mabel Chan

Project Art Editor
Shahid Mahmood

Senior Cartographic Designers
Casper Morris, Suresh Kumar

Cartographer
Jasneet Kaur

DTP Designer
Natasha Lu

Production Controller
Louise Minihane

Photographer
Jon Spaull

Fact Checker
Anastasia Makarova

Picture Credits

t=top; tc=top centre; tr=top right; cla=centre left above; ca=centre above; cra=centre right above; cl=centre left; c=centre; cr=centre right; clb=centre left below; cb=centre below; crb=centre right below; bl=bottom left; bc=bottom centre; br=bottom right.

Every effort has been made to trace the copyright holders, and we apologize in advance for any unintentional omissions. We would be pleased to insert the appropriate acknowledgements in any subsequent edition of this publication.

The photographer, writers and publisher would like to thank the media staff at the following sights and organizations for their helpful cooperation:

Siobhan Bennetts; Dostoevsky House Museum; Professor Viktor Eniseiskiy; Vasilisi Kiyski; Lyuba Krasnoselskaya; Nabokov Museum; Tatiana Nevinskaya; Andrey Smirnov; Alexander Zubkov.

AKG-IMAGES: 32c.

ALAMY IMAGES: Dennis Hallivan 12bl; imagebroker/ Ferdinand Hollweck 20–21; Maurice Joseph 21tr; Michael Klinec 22–23; Jeremy Nicholl 32tr; The Print Collector 32tl, 35cl; Simon Reddy 37clb; Robert Harding Picture Library Limited/Sylvain Grandadam 12tc; Stephen Saks Photography 8–9; Visual Arts Library

(London)/Dmitri Grigor'evich Levitsky, (1735–1822) 13tl.

VALENTIN BARANOVSKY: 2tl, 38tc.

THE BRIDGEMAN ART LIBRARY: 27tc; The State Hermitage Museum, St Petersburg 12tl/tr.

CORBIS: Archivo Iconografico, S.A/Orest A Kiprenski 34tl; Archivo Icongrafico, S.A/Vladimir Egorpvic Makovskij 32br, 33r; Philip Gould 17tr; Michael Nicholson 26br; Charles O'Rear 1; Gianni Dagli Orti 17cr; Steve Raymer 6bl, 16–17; Sygma/ Sophie Bassouls 34tr; Sygma/ Antoine Gyori 30–31, 33bl, 102tl; Bo Zaunders 42–43.

GETTY IMAGES: Digital Vision/ Martin Child 100–101; The Image Bank/ Harald Sund 50bl.

KEA PUBLISHING: Francesco Venturi 6cl.

PICTOR INTERNATIONAL: 7ca.

NATASHA RAZINA: 27cr.

REUTERS: Peter Skingley 34tc.

ELLEN ROONEY: 10–11c.

THE STATE HERMITAGE MUSEUM, ST PETERSBURG: 11br

STATE RUSSIAN MUSEUM: 18cb, 19clb/tr.

All other images © Dorling Kindersley.

For further information see: www.dkimages.com.

Acknowledgements

Special Editions of DK Travel Guides

DK Travel Guides can be purchased in bulk quantities at discounted prices for use in promotions or as premiums. We are also able to offer special editions and personalized jackets, corporate imprints and excerpts from all of our books, tailored specifically to meet your own needs.

To find out more, please contact:

(in the United States) **SpecialSales@dk.com**

(in the UK) **Sarah.Burgess@dk.com**

(in Canada) DK Special Sales at **general@tourmaline.ca**

(in Australia) **business.development@pearson.com.au**

Phrase Book

In this guide the Russian language has been transliterated into Roman script. All street and place names, and the names of most people, are transliterated according to this system. For some names, where a well-known English form exists, this has been used – hence, Leo (not Lev) Tolstoy. In particular, the names of Russian rulers, such as Peter the Great, are given in their anglicized forms. Throughout the book, transliterated names can be taken as an accurate guide to pronunciation. The Phrase Book also gives a phonetic guide to the pronunciation of words and phrases.

Guidelines for Pronunciation

The Cyrillic alphabet has 33 letters, of which only five (a, к, м, о, т) correspond exactly to their counterparts in English. Russian has two pronunciations (hard and soft) of each of its vowels, and several consonants without an equivalent.

The right-hand column of the alphabet, below, demonstrates how Cyrillic letters are pronounced by comparing them to sounds in English words. However, some letters vary in how they are pronounced according to their position in a word. Important exceptions are also noted below.

On the following pages, the English is given in the left-hand column, with the Russian and its transliteration in the middle column. In the Menu Decoder section the Russian is given in the left-hand column and the English translation in the right-hand column, for ease of use. Because there are genders in Russian, in a few cases both masculine and feminine forms of a phrase are given.

THE CYRILLIC ALPHABET

А а	**a**	**a**limony
Б б	**b**	**b**ed
В в	**v**	**v**et
Г г	**g**	**g**et (see note 1)
Д д	**d**	**d**ebt
Е е	**e**	**ye**t (see note 2)
Ё ё	**e**	**yo**nder
Ж ж	**zh**	lei**s**ure (but a little harder)
З з	**z**	**z**ither
И и	**i**	s**ee**
Й й	**y**	bo**y** (see note 3)
К к	**k**	**k**ing
Л л	**l**	**l**oot
М м	**m**	**m**atch
Н н	**n**	**n**ever
О о	**o**	r**o**b (see note 4)
П п	**p**	**p**ea
Р р	**r**	**r**at (rolling, as in Italian)
С с	**s**	**s**top
Т т	**t**	**t**offee
У у	**u**	b**oo**t
Ф ф	**f**	**f**ellow
Х х	**kh**	**kh** (like loch)
Ц ц	**ts**	le**ts**
Ч ч	**ch**	**ch**air
Ш ш	**sh**	**sh**ove
Щ щ	**shch**	fre**sh sh**eet (with a slight roll)
ъ		hard sign (no sound, but **see** note 5)
Ы ы	**y**	l**i**d
ь		soft sign (no sound, but see note 5)
Э э	**e**	**e**gg
Ю ю	**yu**	**you**th
Я я	**ya**	**ya**k

Notes

1) Г Pronounced as v in endings -oro and -ero.
2) Е Always pronounced ye at the beginning of a word, but in the middle of a word sometimes less distinctly (more like e).
3) Й This letter has no distinct sound of its own. It usually lengthens the preceding vowel.
4) О When not stressed it is pronounced like a in a**cross**.
5) ъ, ь The hard sign (ъ) is rare and indicates a very brief pause before the next letter. The soft sign (ь, marked in the pronunciation guide as ') softens the preceding consonant and adds a slight y sound: for instance, n' would sound like ny in 'ca**ny**on'.

In an Emergency

Help!	Помогите!	pamag**ee**t-ye!
	Pomogite!	
Stop!	Стоп!	stop!
	Stop!	
Leave me alone!	Оставьте меня в покое!	ast**a**vt'-ye myen**ya** v pak**oy**e!
	Ostavte menya v pokoe!	
Call a doctor!	Позовите врача!	pazav**ee**t-ye vr**a**cha!
	Pozovite vracha!	
Call an ambulance!	Вызовите скорую помощь!	v**i**zaveet-ye sk**o**ru-yu p**o**mash'!
	Vyzovite skoruyu pomoshch!	
Fire!	Пожар!	pazh**a**r!
	Pozhar!	
Police!	Милиция!	meel**ee**tsee-ya!
	Militsiya!	
Where is the nearest...	Где ближайший...	gdye bleezh**a**ysheey...
...telephone?	...телефон?	...tyelyef**o**n?
	...telefon?	
...hospital?	...больница?	...bal'n**ee**tsa?
	...bolnitsa?	
...police station?	...отделение милиции?	...atdyel**ye**nye meel**ee**tsee-ee?
	...otdelenie militsii?	

Communication Essentials

Yes	Да	da
	Da	
No	Нет	nyet
	Net	
Please	Пожалуйста	pazh**a**lsta
	Pozhaluysta	
Thank you	Спасибо	spas**ee**ba
	Spasibo	
Excuse me	Извините	eezveen**ee**t-ye
	Izvinite	
Hello	Здравствуйте	zdr**a**stvooyt-ye
	Zdravstvuyte	
Goodbye	До свидания	da sveed**a**nya
	Do svidaniya	

What?	Что?	shto?
	Chto?	
Where?	Где?	gdye?
	Gde?	
Wzzzzy?	Почему?	pachyemoo?
	Pochemu?	
When?	Когда?	kagda?
	Kogda?	

Useful Phrases

How are you?	Как Вы Поживаете?	kak vee pozhivaete?
	Kak vee pozhivaete?	
Very well, thank you	Хорошо, спасибо	kharasho, spaseeba,
	Khorosho, spasibo	
Pleased to meet you	Очень приятно	ochen' pree-yatna
	Ochen priyatno	
How do I get to...?	Как добраться до...?	kak dabrat'sya da...?
	Kak dobratsya do...?	
Do you speak English?	Вы говорите по-английски?	vi gavaree-ye po-angleeskee?
	Vy govorite po-angliyski?	
don't understand	Я не понимаю	ya nye paneema-yoo
	Ya ne ponimayu	
am lost	я заблудился (заблудилась)	ya zabloodeelsya (zabloodeelas')
	Ya zabludilsya (zabludilas)	

Useful Words

big	большой	bal'shoy
	bolshoy	
small	маленький	malyen'kee
	malenkiy	
hot (water, food)	горячий	garyachee
	goryachiy	
hot (weather)	жарко	zharka
	zharko	
cold	холодный	khalodnee
	kholodnyy	
good	хорошо	kharasho
	khorosho	
bad	плохо	plokha
	plokho	
early	рано	rana
	rano	
late	поздно	pozdna
	pozdno	
free (no charge)	бесплатно	byesplatna
	besplatno	
toilet	туалет	tooalyet
	tualet	

Eating Out

A table for two, please	Стол на двоих, пожалуйста	stol na dva-eekh, pazhalsta
	Stol na dva pazhalsta	
would like to book a table	Я хочу заказать стол	ya khachoo zakazat' stol
	Ya khochu zakazat stol	
The bill, please	Счёт, пожалуйста	shyot, pazhalsta
	Schet, pozhaluysta	
am a vegetarian	Я вегетарианец (вегетарианка)	ya vyegyetaree-anyets (vyegyetaree-anka)
	Ya vegetarianets (vegetarianka)	
breakfast	завтрак	zaftrak
	zavtrak	

lunch	обед	abyet
	obed	
dinner	ужин	oozheen
	uzhin	
waiter!	официант!	afeetsee-ant!
	ofitsiant!	
waitress!	официантка!	afeetsee-antka!
	ofitsiantka!	
dish of the day	фирменное блюдо	feermenoye blyooda
	firmennoe blyudo	
appetizers/ starters	закуски	zakooskee
	zakuski	
main course	второе блюдо	ftaroye blyooda
	vtoroe blyudo	
meat and poultry dishes	мясные блюда	myasniye blyooda
	myasnye blyuda	
fish and seafood dishes	рыбные блюда	ribniye blyooda
	rybnye blyuda	
vegetable dishes	овощные блюда	avashshniye blyooda
	ovoshchnye blyuda	
dessert	десерт	dyesyert
	desert	
drinks	напитки	napeetkee
	napitki	
vegetables	овощи	ovashshee
	ovoshchi	
bread	хлеб	khlyeb
	khleb	
wine list	карта вин	karta veen
	karta vin	
glass	стакан	stakan
	stakan	
bottle	бутылка	bootilka
	butylka	
salt	соль	sol'
	sol	
pepper	перец	pyeryets
	perets	
butter/oil	масло	masla
	maslo	
sugar	сахар	sakhar
	sakhar	

Menu Decoder

белое вино	byelaye veeno	white wine
beloe vino		
варёный	varyonee	boiled
varenyy		
вода	vada	water
voda		
жареный	zharyenee	roasted/grilled/ fried
zharenyy		
икра	eekra	black caviar
ikra		
икра красная/ кета	eekra krasna-ya/ kyeta	red caviar
ikra krasnaya/ keta		
красное вино	krasnoye veeno	red wine
krasnoe vino		
курица	kooreetsa	chicken
kuritsa		
лук	look	onion
luk		
минеральная вода	mineral'naya vada	mineral water
mineralnaya voda		
мороженое	marozhena-ye	ice-cream
morozhenoe		

мясо	myasa	meat
myaso		
печёнка	pyechyonka	liver
pechenka		
печёный	pyechyonee	baked
pechenyy		
пиво	peeva	beer
pivo		
помидор	pameedor	tomato
pomidor		
морепродукты	moryeproduktee	seafood
moryeproduktee		
рыба	riba	fish
ryba		
салат	salat	salad
salat		
сосиски	saseeskee	sausages
sosiski		
сыр	sir	cheese
syr		
сырой	siroy	raw
syroy		
чеснок	chyesnok	garlic
chesnok		
яйцо	yaytso	egg
yaytso		
фрукты	frookti	fruit
frukty		

Staying in a Hotel

Do you have a vacant room?	У вас есть свободный номер?	oo vas yest' svabodnee nomyer?
	U vas yest svobodnyy nomer?	
single room	одноместный номер	adnamyestnee nomyer
	odnomestnyy nomer	
double room with double bed	номер с двуспальной кроватью	nomyer s dvoospal'noy kravat'-yoo
	nomer s dvuspalnoy krovatyu	
key	ключ	klyooch
	klyuch	

Time, Days and Dates

one minute	одна минута	adna meenoota
	odna minuta	
one hour	час	chas
	chas	
half an hour	полчаса	polchasa
	polchasa	
day	день	dyen'
	den	
week	неделя	nyedyel-ya
	nedelya	
Monday	понедельник	panyedyel'neek
	ponedelnik	
Tuesday	вторник	ftorneek
	vtornik	
Wednesday	среда	sryeda
	sreda	
Thursday	четверг	chyetvyerk
	chetverg	
Friday	пятница	pyatneetsa
	pyatnitsa	
Saturday	суббота	soobota
	subbota	
Sunday	воскресенье	vaskryesyen'ye
	voskresene	

Numbers

1	один/одна/одно	adeen/adna/adno
	odin/odna/odno	
2	два/две	dva/dvye
	dva/dve	
3	три	tree
	tri	
4	четыре	chyetir-ye
	chetyre	
5	пять	pyat'
	pyat	
6	шесть	shest'
	shest	
7	семь	syem'
	sem	
8	восемь	vosyem'
	vosem	
9	девять	dyevyat'
	devyat	
10	десять	dyesyat'
	desyat	
11	одиннадцать	adeenatsat'
	odinnadtsat	
12	двенадцать	dvyenatsat'
	dvenadtsat	
13	тринадцать	treenatsat'
	trinadtsat	
14	четырнадцать	chyetirnatsat'
	chetyrnadtsat	
15	пятнадцать	pyatnatsat'
	pyatnadtsat	
16	шестнадцать	shestnatsat'
	shestnadtsat	
17	семнадцать	syemnatsat'
	semnadtsat	
18	восемнадцать	vasyemnatsat'
	vosemnadtsat	
19	девятнадцать	dyevyatnatsat'
	devyatnadtsat	
20	двадцать	dvatsat'
	dvadtsat	
30	тридцать	treetsat'
	tridtsat	
40	сорок	sorak
	sorok	
50	пятьдесят	pyadyesyat'
	pyatdesyat	
60	шестьдесят	shes'dyesyat
	shestdesyat	
70	семьдесят	syem'dyesyat
	semdesyat	
80	восемьдесят	vosyem'dyesyat
	vosemdesyat	
90	девяносто	dyevyanosta
	devyanosto	
100	сто	sto
	sto	
200	двести	dvyestee
	dvesti	
300	триста	treesta
	trista	
400	четыреста	chyetiryesta
	chetyresta	
500	пятьсот	pyat'sot
	pyatsot	
1,000	тысяча	tisyacha
	tysyacha	
2,000	две тысячи	dvye tisyachi
	dve tysyachi	
5,000	пять тысяч	pyat' tisyach
	pyat tysyach	
1,000,000	миллион	meelee-on
	million	